MISHAP OR MURDER?

TRUE TALES OF MYSTERIOUS DEATHS AND DISAPPEARANCES

EILEEN ORMSBY

CONTENTS

MORE BOOKS AND FREEBIES

WHAT CRITICS HAVE SAID ABOUT EILEEN ORMSBY'S BOOKS

"Ormsby has delivered a triumph of narrative journalism, meticulously researched and gripping, a skilful mergence of tech jargon with human drama." *The Saturday Paper*

"The book is a fascinating expose of this particular aspect of the "dark web" of internet dealings and its subsequent unravelling." *Sydney Morning Herald*

"Ormsby's investigative journalism shines as she provides a very thorough account of Ulbricht's rise and fall." *Penthouse Magazine*

"What pulls you through The Darkest Web isn't its often-nefarious, sometimes-gory details, but Ormsby's handling of three progressively intense narrative arcs." *The Guardian*

"The darknet has become a repository for human cruelty, perversion and psychosis, and Ormsby captures all the tragedy in her gripping book." *The Australian*

"A great strength of the meticulously researched Silk Road is the manner in which Ormsby gently takes the reader by the hand, unpacking the technology underpinning this 'dark net' market." *Australian Police Journal*

"A disillusioned corporate lawyer turned writer from Australia, Eileen's new book, The Darkest Web, is the story of her journey, from drug markets and contract killing sites to the Internet's seediest alcoves. But the most startling moments of the book happen when she comes face-to-face with some of its key players." *VICE*

"From the Internet's hidden drug dens to torture-porn websites, Ormsby has seen it all. If you've ever wondered what the Dark Web is really like, Darkest Web should be on your TBR." *Bustle Magazine: The Best New True Crime Books You Can Read Right Now*

"Riveting." *Who Magazine*

"Investigative journalism that gallops along at a cracking pace." *SMH Good Weekend*

"Through her clear rendering of the facts, Ormsby makes the intricacies of the technology involved accessible to even the most technophobic of readers. The tone is conversational and friendly while the content is intriguing and increasingly dark. In her quest to uncover the mystery behind the enigmatic DPR she uncovers a story of subterfuge, replete with conspiracy theories and hidden identities, that is rich with anecdotes." *Newtown Review of Books*

"Ormsby is a great writer, giving us gripping accounts from the people who actually used "Silk Road" to paint an accurate picture of how the website was created, run, and ultimately fell . . . Silk Road is easily one of the best books I've read this year." *The Library NZ*

"Silk Road is one of the more readable and gripping true crime books of recent times. It is not just Ormsby's knowledge of the brief but spectacular rise and fall of Silk Road that makes for compelling reading, but also the ordering of the material so that the reader has the sense of being educated in the technical and legal background to an astonishing criminal enterprise." *The Australian*

"For the most complete account of the original Silk Road ... Eileen Ormsby's book Silk Road is the best place to start. It's full of original research, interviews and insight. This is best read along with her excellent blog, AllThingsVice, which covers several aspects of the dark net, but especially the dark net markets." *Jamie Bartlett, author of Darknet and Radicals*

"[*Stalkers* is] chilling... harrowing...unpicks the sordid tale from the start" *The Sun*

"Dark, disturbing and near unbelievable... [*Stalkers* is] my No.1 true crime read this year" *OzNoir*

ABOUT THE AUTHOR

Eileen Ormsby is a lawyer, author and freelance journalist based in Melbourne. Her first book, "Silk Road" was the world's first in-depth expose of the black markets that operate on the dark web. In "The Darkest Web", Eileen's gonzo-style investigations led her deep into the secretive corners of the dark web where drugs and weapons dealers, hackers, hitmen and worse ply their trade. Many of these dark web interactions turned into real-world relationships, entanglements, hack attempts on her computer and even death threats from the dark web's most successful hitman network.

Eileen started writing scripts for the Casefile True Crime Podcast in 2018 and has since become one of their most regular contributors. She often focuses on cases that have a dark web or internet aspect to them.

ALSO BY EILEEN ORMSBY

A Manual for Murder: FREE AND EXCLUSIVE

Psycho.com: serial killers on the internet

Murder on the Dark Web: true stories from the dark side of the internet

Stalkers: true tales of deadly obsessions

Little Girls Lost: true tales of heinous crimes

The Darkest Web

Silk Road

Sneak peeks of these books and a link to get your FREE TRUE CRIME BOOK at the end of this book

INTRODUCTION

They are questions that most of us have contemplated at some time: How many people have managed to get away with murder, without anyone ever discovering a crime has been committed? What really happened to those people who disappeared into thin air, vanishing without a trace? How often does a death get miscategorized as an accident or suicide when more sinister forces are at play? Was it mishap… or murder?

Premature deaths happen every day. An accident or a sudden unexpected illness or condition such as an aneurysm or heart attack can take a loved one in the blink of an eye. Police and paramedics are called to the scenes of suicides and homicides with depressing regularity. Usually, these professionals don't take long to establish whether a particular death was a tragic accident, a solo affair, or if somebody else was involved. Most murders are solved almost as soon as they occur: there will generally be some sort of violence involved and a few pertinent questions will unveil a history between the victim and somebody else that makes homicide a more likely explanation than a clumsy victim falling and hitting their head. Police usually do not have far to look for a culprit, with spouses being the most obvious and common perpetrators.

But what if the cause of death is not as obvious as a stab wound, bullet, or strangulation? There are poisons that mimic the symptoms of a heart attack or other medical conditions. If the victim is elderly, overweight, or otherwise in a high-risk category, their death may not be investigated very carefully. When two people are walking along a clifftop, it can be nearly impossible to tell if one of them slipped in a tragic accident or was pushed by their companion. A house fire that ends tragically might be a cover-up for a sinister plot. How can you tell if someone was strangled or died of smoke inhalation if all you have are their charred remains? And what if there is no body at all? In any given year, hundreds of thousands of people disappear seemingly into thin air in the US, UK, and Australia. Worldwide, the number is estimated to be in the millions.

An investigation may not even be opened up unless there are other clues—a dissatisfied marriage, an affair, a large insurance claim may all point to the fall or the illness or the disappearance not being quite as random as it seemed. If motives are present—if someone stands to profit or is prone to jealousy—an unexpected death is more likely to be scrutinized. Of course, many people have a multitude of motives to kill but never carry through on their plan.

When a homicide or disappearance goes unsolved for

many years, it is possible that a diabolical genius carried out the perfect murder and managed to cover his or her tracks flawlessly afterwards. Possible... but unlikely. The real reason many murders and disappearances have gone unsolved or undetected is more mundane. Overworked or inexperienced police simply might not have found the murderer. They check the obvious sources of evidence for the suspects, enter the information into their databases and move onto the next case. Sometimes they don't have any decent suspects. The woman found dead in her flat, for example, didn't have any reason to be killed, had no family, and was liked by her neighbors. Sometimes the crime simply does not seem to be worth the time of an investigator, especially if there is no obvious lead. Dozens of murders might go unreported and undocumented each year. And if they occur in a place with little or no media interest, where the nearest police station is a couple of hours away, overworked and underfunded, the chance of anyone noticing or recording these events is remote.

Some people get away with murder because of lack of evidence. Advances in DNA testing have allowed cold cases to be revisited and closed, solving ancient crimes. But there are others that have no DNA—it may have been burned in a fire, scattered in the sea, or lost over time when it was supposed to be kept in safe custody.

Sometimes the circumstances of a crime are complicated by other factors or events that may or may not be related, making investigating the crime more difficult for police. In one tragic case, toddler Jaidyn Leskie was reported to have been kidnapped in 1997 while in the care of his mother's boyfriend. Police were immediately suspicious of the boyfriend, Greg Domaszewicz, who was known to be aggressive and unstable, but on that same evening, the house had been vandalized by persons unknown, culminating with a pig's head being thrown through the window. Jaidyn came from a troubled background and had an erratic life. He was brought up in poverty by people with little formal education or employment prospects, exacerbated by drug use and a life of violence. Jaidyn's body was found six months later, but his murder remains unsolved.

In very rare cases, a case will go unsolved because of a conspiracy to protect the killer. This was the case in the 1981 murder of Ken Rex McElroy from Skidmore, Missouri. McElroy was the town bully, but his crimes went far beyond calling people names or kicking sand in their faces. McElroy was a repeat felon whose crimes included assault, child molestation, statutory rape, arson, animal cruelty, hog and cattle rustling, and burglary. The people of Skidmore were terrified of McElroy, who had made the lives of most of the townsfolk unbearable over the years.

When he was gunned down in broad daylight in a crowded place, nobody called an ambulance. Afterwards, every witness claimed to be looking the other way and none were able to identify the gunman. No charges were ever pressed and the townsfolk seemed to agree that justice had been served.

There are many high-profile examples of unsolved murders and disappearances. Entire multi-season Netflix series have spawned water cooler debates about whether Jon-Benet's brother was involved, who abducted Maddie, or what happened to Maura. Online communities, such as Websleuths and Reddit spend hours, days and months examining every microscopic aspect of these mysteries, dissecting news and law enforcement reports, looking for clues that investigators might have missed. These are the sorts of cases that nearly everybody has an opinion about and are often the subject of heated arguments.

But there are many other disappearances and deaths that don't garner as much attention. This book takes a deep dive into some lesser-known but equally baffling cases. The circumstances surrounding some of these cases are so bizarre they could be a made-for-TV movie script.

The first is a current and ongoing mystery about a missing couple in Australia's High Country. Normally, the story of an elderly couple going missing while camping would warrant only a few news stories before fading away as a tragic, yet not uncommon, mishap. But throw in an illicit septuagenarian affair, a missing drone, a burned-out campsite, rumors of serial killers, and a mysterious loner known as "the Button Man," and this is a story that has kept Australia intrigued for over a year.

In the second story, young skydiver Stephen Hilder was killed in a very obvious and deliberate parachute sabotage event. There was no way it was accidental. There was also no doubt that his killer was a skydiver who attended the competition Stephen was jumping in that weekend. But detectives found themselves out of their depth in a world filled with adrenaline junkies in a high-stakes sport.

The third case in this book is similar to that of the hated McElroy. There was not much by way of forensics in his Australian country town in the 1970s when Russell

Martin went missing. Many people had a motive to kill him and witnesses may have remained silent for decades

The final case of Daniella Vian is one of those cases where unusual factors that may or may not be connected to her disappearance complicated the investigation. Daniella's exact movements were recorded by her car's GPS and text messages right up to the moment of her disappearance, but still police were unable to locate her or her car after a night out for what should have been a celebration.

How many murders have gone undetected? We probably will never know the true statistics, but these cold cases will keep you wondering.

HIGH COUNTRY MISADVENTURE

THE DISAPPEARANCE OF RUSSELL HILL AND CAROL CLAY

A CLANDESTINE TRIP

O n March 19, 2020, at around 7 a.m., 74-year-old Russell Hill left his house in Drouin, Victoria, Australia, and drove thirty minutes to pick up his 73-year-old friend, Carol Clay, from her brand-new house in Pakenham. The two septuagenarians were embarking on a camping trip in the Wonnangatta Valley, around 120 miles to the north-east of the state, with plans to visit various campsites along the Dargo River.

Russell's recent-model Toyota LandCruiser 4WD was the perfect vehicle for the trip, able to navigate the roughest terrain. He had set up the pickup truck to be the perfect camping companion. Everything he needed was set within the metal canopy that took up the entire tray of the truck. The sides opened up to show storage, shelves, and a kitchen. The experienced bushman and former logger was also an amateur, or "ham," radio enthusiast, known to string wires up in the trees around his campsite leading to an antenna in order to get a signal and chat to any of the tight-knit group of fellow enthusiasts who were some of his closest friends. He was also keen to practice flying his new Mavic model drone that he had brought along. It was an expensive device for a beginner, worth a couple of thousand dollars. Russell called his drone "Fred." A high-end hobbyist drone, the Mavic comes with a steep learning curve and is hard to control at first. Most people need to practice for several hours in open areas to get used to it.

This would be Russell's third trip to the area in a month. He had gone camping just a week before, in the area of the King Billy and Bluff Track, apparently alone. The trip surprised his friends, because it was a six-hour drive each way, which seemed excessive for a one-night stay. He had been trying out flying and filming with his drone there.

Carol was a former president of the Country Women's Association. She was so well-known for her baking that she was in high demand for lessons and demonstrations, sharing her secrets of short crust and filo pastry, or the perfect Christmas cake. She also worked on a diverse range of programs and was determined to break the view that the CWA was only about old ladies knitting and baking, actively trying to recruit junior members. The CWA, Carol told the *Pakenham Gazette* on the Association's eighty-fifth birthday, was "a modern organisation of women looking out for women." Her time as president saw her being invited to Government House, she traveled Australia and the South Pacific to attend conferences and sat on the boards and round tables of some high-profile organizations. Carol was a powerhouse.

Carol had been inducted as a Member of Honour of the Country Women's Association in 2018. She was the sort of woman who could teach you to make home-made jams, pickles and pesto from your garden's summer harvest, or curate an exhibition promoting members' artworks for National Science Week.

"We are always connected with tea and scones, so to be associated with a science project is quite exciting," Carol told a reporter from one of Victoria's major news-papers, *The Age*. If she had committed to a task, she would stay up to the wee hours of the morning making sure that last cake was cooked or pudding soaked. If a friend was sick, Carol would be there every day, dropping off hearty cooked dinners until they got better.

Carol's community service went beyond her work in the CWA to volunteering with hospital auxiliaries and the Red Cross, as well as sitting on various kindergarten, school, and tennis club committees. But she was also known to take a lot of pride in how she looked—a "glamor queen" one friend said. Her children had grown up and had children of their own, and Carol doted on her grandchildren, proudly showing the latest photos, and exclaiming over their newest accomplishments. She had recently downsized her living arrangements to a new house that was conveniently close to shops and train station.

Carol and Russell had known each other for most of their lives. Russell and his wife, Robyn, had attended Carol's first wedding some fifty years earlier. This trip, however, was a clandestine one. Neither Robyn nor Carol's family knew that they were camping together. Russell had told Robyn that he was going camping alone, which he did often. Carol, who had been single for several years and lived alone, told friends that she was going away for a few days, without specifying where. She asked her neighbors to water her plants. She told them to expect her back by March 29.

Many people who knew the glamorous Carol would be surprised to find that she had gone camping at all. She was never without her signature bright red lipstick and was always carefully dressed. Nobody had ever seen her in anything as casual as track pants. Her steel-gray hair was stylishly cut in the fashion of ladies of a certain age so that it showed off the pearl earrings she almost always wore.

It wasn't their first clandestine tryst to the bush. The previous month they had camped at Pike's Flat, also in the area known as the Victoria's High Country, and they had been away on several trips before that. Russell had also taken Carol on logging truck journeys before he retired.

That Thursday morning, Carol's neighbors saw Russell putting Carol's bags in the trunk of his car. Then the couple set off together, heading for Victoria's High Country.

SETTING UP CAMP

With its panoramic views and challenging 4WD tracks, the trip to the Wonnangatta Valley is considered one of the iconic drives in the Victorian High Country. Russell and Carol drove through Licola, a small town on the banks of the Macalister River, before commencing the more challenging part of the trip, characterized by tracks that can only be accessed with an all-terrain vehicle.

That night, they set up camp at Howitt Hut at Howitt Plains, a basic campground popular with horse trail riders thanks to stockyards where horses could be safely penned in for the night. Howitt Hut, almost derelict under a corrugated iron roof, was one of the many huts of the High Country, built in the early 1900s. It was not their final destination, but rather somewhere convenient to camp overnight before heading into more rugged bushland when they had plenty of daylight.

The next day, they took the Zeka Spur Track, recommended for 4WD vehicles only, into some of the most remote terrain the state of Victoria has to offer. Although the bush is thick going in, the campsite they chose was in a flat open area in a valley, ideal for setting up camp and flying the drone. It was a spot on Dry River Track, a popular path for bushwalkers and horse riders, and the route that drovers took their cattle from the Wonnangatta Station to the Howitt Plains for summer grazing before the station was closed and the area became a national park. The campsite sat at the junction of the Dry River and the Wonnangatta River, a short walk from one of the long-drop toilets that serviced campers in the area.

That evening, at around 6 p.m., amateur radio enthusiast Russell joined his friends on their usual ham radio hookup. The group, which included his best mate, Rob Ashlin, got together most nights on the frequency 3.675. Russell's call sign was VK3 VZP. It was a social thing, but also a way of checking in with each other, especially when they were out bush and out of cell phone range. Russell said he couldn't talk for long, as he was setting up camp and it would be dark soon. He also mentioned that he was having trouble with his radio. Nevertheless, he sounded upbeat and positive. He promised he would call in again the next evening at the same time as usual. He didn't mention that he was camping with Carol. Most of his friends were old-fashioned, and some knew Russell's wife Robyn, and would not approve of the situation.

Friends called Russell a fastidious camper who knew exactly what he had and where it was stored. He would tidy things away and put them back in their assigned spots. Like many camping enthusiasts, he had put together the perfect configuration over the years, and every time he camped, the setup was the same. His 2017 70-series Toyota LandCruiser was considered by many 4WD enthusiasts as a premium off-road vehicle. He was safety-conscious and aware of the dangers that lurked in the rugged and unforgiving Australian bushland. His single-cab truck was specifically set up for camping, and he was proud of it.

Carol, on the other hand, was not the sort of person that people imagined would enjoy camping at all. She probably let Russell set up their site just the way he liked it—tent with an awning, a separate toilet/shower tent placed a few feet away, fold-up chairs and a table. Carol's job would have been preparing and cooking the food, a task at which she excelled.

The picturesque Wonnangatta Valley, with its rolling hills and challenging hiking tracks, is part of the Alpine National Park. It's a nice place to visit, and a nice place to walk, and—importantly for these campers—secluded and private. The paths in and out of the valley could be treacherous, meandering into the bush via steep and rugged terrain, rocky with thick undergrowth and plenty of places to potentially get hurt.

Not far away from where Russell and Carol set up camp was Wonnangatta Station, infamous for being the scene of a dramatic and still unsolved murder mystery in the early 1900s. Books and historical plaques placed around the area regale the tale of the cattle station manager who was shot dead, and the station cook who was the prime suspect. The cook was not tried for the crime, and several months later he too was found with a bullet in his head. The murders remain unsolved to this day.

They were not the last mysterious deaths to occur in this section of Victoria's High Country.

MYSTERIES OF THE HIGH COUNTRY

"This is very unforgiving Australian bush, it can swallow people up."
– Greg Paul, Victoria Police Search and Rescue Squad, press conference, May 1, 2020

The High Country, as it is known, is an area in north-east Victoria, Australia, of mountainous bushland and rivers that range from raging to a trickle, depending on the time of year. The rugged country was made famous by *The Man From Snowy River*, first a poem by laureate Banjo Patterson, then later a successful Australian film starring Kirk Douglas and Tom Burlinson. It is known as brumby (wild horse) country and for its horse trails, dirt bike riding, hiking, and fishing. It is rich in history, with tales of brumby-wrangling cattlemen and bushrangers during the goldrush era. It is home to Victoria's highest mountains and is used for skiing during the winter season. Many parts of the High

Country become completely inaccessible during the colder months and the tracks are closed off to visitors.

There are dozens of campsites, ranging from large, popular ones that are not far off the road and have mobile phone coverage and toilets that are cleaned regularly, to those that are walk-in only, for more adventurous campers. It is popular for fishing, horse-riding, and hiking, but rumor has it that it is also home to several illegal cannabis plantations and other nefarious activities. The bush is so dense that they can be easily hidden from nosy neighbors, and even helicopters and drones.

It's an area where thousands of people go camping every year without incident. At worst, the family dog might be bitten by a snake or a child suffer mosquito bites or the sting of a Christmas beetle. But it is also an area where there have been several mysterious disappearances over the years.

In 2008, father of two and experienced hiker Warren Myer took off from Dom Dom Saddle parking lot for a six-mile walk. He was well prepared, with a fully charged phone, GPS, food, and water. He has never been seen since. A State Emergency Services volunteer said, "Although it was rough terrain through the area ... it didn't seem an impossible spot and if he truly was as careful as we've been led to believe (and as experienced) it did seem very odd ... I was there for some of the search and know firsthand there was simply no clue anywhere ... no indication. It was like he'd never existed!"

Police later speculated that Warren had stumbled across an illegal marijuana plantation and was murdered and buried in the bush with earthmoving equipment.

However, no arrests were made, nor persons of interest identified.

In 2011, former governor of Barwon Prison, David Prideaux, disappeared while on a hunting trip with his brother-in-law in Alpine National Park. Barwon was one of the toughest prisons in the country and many people speculated his disappearance had something to do with the recent murder of notorious inmate Carl Williams. Following an inquest, the coroner found no evidence of foul play and ruled it likely that David died from a serious accident or medical causes. His body has never been found.

In July 2019, 72-year-old Conrad Whitlock's car was found near the ski fields of Mount Buller. The strangest thing was that he had no reason to be out there. He hadn't told anyone he was going and he would not have been up to hiking in the area due to his ill-health. He was scheduled to have scans done because he'd been suffering from headaches. He may have become disorientated, possibly due to the medical affliction he was experiencing, and either fell or walked into the bushland and succumbed to the elements. It is unlikely he could have made it far in that terrain if he had a medical episode, and the search and rescue teams found nothing. Some speculated that wild dogs could have disposed of the body. A massive manhunt found no trace of him.

In October 2019, fit and experienced hiker 39-year-old Niels Becker disappeared after setting out on a solo five-day hike in the Alpine National Park. He had reportedly been preparing for the hike for months and was familiar with the Victorian High Country. A team of police and volunteers scoured the area, but no sign of Niels was found. It's possible that he fell, got lost, or was injured and perished due to exposure. Inexperienced hikers can quickly succumb to the elements in the dense and unforgiving High Country. It would not take long for hypothermia to set in. If the local wildlife found a body, it could be torn apart, eaten, and taken far away, making finding the corpse near impossible.

However, when bodies are never found, relatives and police are left with the unsettling possibility that the disappearances may have more sinister explanations. Moreover, when there are several unexplained disappearances in a particular area, the public begins to ask whether it is possible a serial killer is roaming the mountains.

A BURNED-OUT CAMPSITE

At around 2 p.m. on March 21, 2020, a hiker who had been camping at another spot near the Wonnangatta Station came across an unusual scene. At a remote campground at Dry River Track, a pile of ash and the twisted remains of barely recognizable camping equipment formed a blackened pyramid next to a scorched, but otherwise undamaged, 4WD vehicle.

The fire had been severe, obliterating chairs, awning, tent, and everything in it. Flames had licked the nearby white LandCruiser, blackening part of its white exterior, but the damage appeared to be superficial. A toilet tent set up nearby had escaped the inferno.

There was no smoke or smouldering embers, and the ash was cold to the touch, suggesting the fire had been out for several hours at least. The car was locked and nobody seemed to be about.

There were no clues to what had happened. Perhaps there had been a second car, which took the unfortunate campers back out of the unforgiving bush where they could get supplies or extra help, or have any burns attended to. There wasn't much the hiker could do. It was a several-hour drive to any phone reception, and he was on foot. He continued on his hike, which would eventually take him back to where his family was camping.

A FEW MILES AWAY—PERHAPS earlier, perhaps later—men on a bulldozer crew working on the roads were startled when a white twin-cab pickup truck came roaring up the track from Wonnangatta, driving erratically. Hoons were not unknown in the area, but the tracks generally commanded a certain amount of respect from drivers. Many blind corners and sections where cars coming from opposite directions could not pass each other without one backing up first meant that most people took it easy driving in and out of the rugged bush.

Another road crew were annoyed to discover that diesel had been siphoned from their machines. This is a relatively common petty crime by campers or hunters who had not thought to bring extra fuel, or just wanted to save a few dollars. The crew didn't think much of it at the time.

A DAY or two after the hiker came across the scene, a man who was camping in the area with his young son also came across the burned-out campsite. The father thought the scene looked decidedly off and determined that he would alert the authorities as soon as he could. Somewhere nearby he noticed a fluorescent green crossbow arrow, sometimes used by deer hunters in the area. It only barely registered on his radar at the time, as such items were not unusual in the area. When he returned to town, he alerted both the Sale and Myrtleford police about what he had found. The timing of his reports is not clear, but he later told the Melbourne daily newspaper, *Herald-Sun*, that the two police stations had not communicated with each other about his findings.

None of these sightings and reports can be pinned down to specific times, but rough estimates can be established from the information later collated by investigators.

REPORTED MISSING

Russell's amateur radio group was a little concerned when he failed to call at the usual time the next day, but it was not unheard of. He may have had equipment trouble, or simply forgotten. He had mentioned the day before that he was having radio transmission problems and perhaps he hadn't had the opportunity to address them.

When he didn't call the next two days either, however, they became worried. He was so entrenched in the group remote radio comms enthusiasts, that during the scheduled group chat, the members would call out jokingly, asking Russell if he was there, or if he had fallen asleep. Russell didn't answer.

After several days of radio silence, Russell's best friend and fellow ham radio devotee, Rob Ashlin, contacted his wife Robyn, asking if she had heard from him. Robyn's last contact with Russell was via the ham radio on the same evening as his conversation with Rob.

When Russell didn't return on March 27, she reported him missing.

Also on March 27, a camper came forward to tell police that they had come across the burned-out campsite and could tell police where to find it. He led them to the remains of the fire, which police sifted through trying to identify any objects among the rubble. Some pieces of twisted metal could be identified as camp chairs and another piece of metal was clearly once a gas cannister. However, most of the couple's belongings had been burned to the point they were unrecognizable. The Land-Cruiser was locked, but the police noticed that the contents of wallets were strewn around in the footwell.

When police broke in and searched the vehicle, they discovered personal belongings of both Russell Hill and Carol Clay, leading them to surmise that the two were together. The alarm had not yet been raised about Carol, who had told friends she would be back around March 29.

After consulting with the families of both Russell and Carol, Victoria Police put out a call on March 29, appealing to the public to help find the elderly pair. Inspector Craig Gaffee said, "The information we have is that they quite often go camping together. They left on Thursday March 19 with a plan of camping in that area and coming back this weekend. Normally Mr. Hill contacts friends or relatives daily, but that hasn't happened for a number of days now. In relation to the lack of contact, their age, and medical issues around Mr. Hill, we have some concerns for their welfare."

The CWA put out a statement expressing concern for their missing member and urging members to contact police if they knew anything. Carol's car had not moved from the garage at her Pakenham home.

Robyn Hill revealed to newspapers that she had believed Russell was going camping alone. The apparent scandal involving the septuagenarians fueled the tabloid interest in the mystery surrounding the missing couple.

It was not immediately obvious what had caused the fire, and the scene was now several days old. It was impossible to tell how much it had been disturbed. The portable cooler under the car was not singed, and neither were the car tires, suggesting that the fire had burned fast and hot, which would normally point to some sort of accelerant being used. Notably, there was no sign of phones, nor of Russell's new drone, among the debris.

Those who knew Russell said that he was very aware of the dangers of fire in the dense bushland and would never light one too close to the tent, nor would he have left a fire unattended.

Although there was no immediate evidence of an accelerant, investigators found evidence of gas canisters in the debris. Again, Russell's friend insisted there was no chance that Russell would have stored the canisters in his tent. He cooked outside, and gas was always stored in the same place inside his vehicle. Another theory was that a battery system was set up to charge electronic devices and that it may have sparked the fire. However, experienced campers would usually do so in the rear canopy of the vehicle, and not in the tent.

There was no sign of Russell's rugged bushman's boots, nor of any sleeping bags, remnants of which, such as the zippers, would almost certainly survive a fire. Not all campers use sleeping bags, however, and an item such as a comforter could be completely obliterated if the fire burned hot enough. Couples, particularly older couples, are more likely to use regular bedding than to climb in and out of sleeping bags.

The toilet at their campsite had been unused, suggesting the pair had only spent a short amount of time in the area before their deaths. Carol, in particular, was not the type of person who would squat in the bushes when the need arose.

It was apparent that Russell and Carol had been absent from their camp for several days. Police would need to move quickly if there was any hope of locating them.

AN INTENSIVE SEARCH

"I have to say that it's unlikely that we will find them alive."
- Detective Inspector Andrew Stamper, Missing Persons
Squad, press conference May 1 2020

W hen the calls for information yielded no
results, search and rescue efforts started in
earnest. Police used drones and helicopters
to scour the area from above, and the dog squad, along
with experienced mountain cattlemen on horseback,
combed the ground looking for any sign of the missing
couple.

Investigators assumed that the couple had wandered
into the bush and become lost. The scrub was so dense
that it could swallow up even the most experienced bushman. Russell's missing drone and controller caused
searchers to wonder if he had lost control of it and

followed it off the path in search of the expensive piece of equipment, with Carol following. The drone became an intense focus of the search. Any data it had collected had not been uploaded to the cloud as yet, as the valley was well and truly out of cellular range.

By April 3, the search had to be called off due to inclement weather. Efforts were further hampered by the introduction of strict restrictions placed on the search parties due to the COVID-19 outbreak. Police broke the news to the public and made another appeal for information.

A social media post by the CWA said: "Gippsland Hills Group members are deeply saddened by the unsolved mystery of the disappearance of Carol Clay, Member of Honour of the Country Women's Association of Victoria Inc., past State President, past Group President of Gippsland Hills Group, past member of Berry's Creek Branch. Carol is very much loved, admired and respected for her warmth, dedication and passion for CWA. We miss her so much. Carol's family has been informed that the search has been called off, the case remains open, and two detectives are assigned to the case. We extend our love and concern at this time of uncertainty to Carol's family, to the members of her Pakenham Branch and all her CWA friends in Victoria and around Australia, and to the family of her travel companion Russell Hill."

Search efforts were hampered by the remoteness of the area and were very dependent on the weather. Heavy rain and high winds could be too treacherous for any but the most experienced search and rescue teams, and they usually rely on volunteers. The lack of communications also made searching difficult. And, as if that didn't make the search effort difficult enough, they weren't able to take in busloads of volunteers like they would normally do for an intensive search covering a significant area, due to the COVID-19 restrictions on large gatherings that were still being imposed by law. Nevertheless, Victoria Police was supported by a number of organizations—volunteer groups and local government, and non-government agencies—all determined to find the missing couple, preferably alive.

The last known time that Russell and Carol were seen was in Carol's driveway the morning they had set off for their trip. There were no sightings of them in the Wonnangatta Valley, which struck searchers as unusual, because their disappearance had happened in the lead-up to a weekend and the weather was good, which would usually mean many people heading to the area for four-wheel driving, hunting, and bushwalking. The tracks to the valley were single lane, meaning that if a car was driving in or out and there was another coming the other way, one of them would have to pull over to let the other pass. On the one hand, Russell's 2017 single-cab 70-series LandCruiser was an impressive car among enthusiasts, and it was likely that those who passed would remember it. On the other hand, a white 4WD was the most common type of vehicle in the area and would not have been noticed by most campers who didn't have a special interest in cars.

Ten days of searching with the coordinated effort with multiple agencies came up with nothing. No phones, no drone, and no Russell or Carol.

ONCE THE WEATHER CLEARED, the search was reignited on April 14. This time searchers focused on more rugged terrain in the region. As it was over three weeks since the pair went missing, investigators did not expect to find them alive, but hoped to find some clue that would bring closure to their families.

One of the avenues police had to consider was whether the illicit lovers had simply run off together to start a new life together. However, they quickly discounted this possibility. Both of them were financially secure, with strong networks of friends and family that they were close to and unlikely to leave behind. Investigators surmised that they had been carrying on their affair for some years, picking up after having been teenage sweethearts over half a century earlier. There was no evidence of a second car, nor that their phones had come back into range (which would have been picked up with police telco searches), nor had any bank accounts been used. Although there were some vague sightings of elderly couples who resembled the pair, nothing of substance was provided to investigators. Even if the idea had been plausible, it would have been nearly impossible for them to pull it off.

Police were confident the pair did not fake their own deaths and did not believe it was a case of murder-suicide.

On April 22, the search was once again called off. There were no leads or results, conclusive or otherwise. The police once again fronted the media to appeal for information but were blunt in advising the public that they did not expect to find Russell and Carol alive. Detective Inspector Andrew Stamper of the Missing Persons Squad told the gathered reporters that they could not rule out foul play, but nor could they state that for certain that foul play was involved.

Police were able to discern the route they took up to the Zeta Spur Track, which took them into the Wonnangatta Valley, by tracing their cell phones. However, once they entered the remote bushland, all phone signals were lost. The detective urged anyone in the public who might have dash cam or hunting cam footage, farm cameras or CCTV in the area, to come forward.

An added complication was that some people who had been camping in the area might be reluctant to come forward lest they would be subject to fines for breaching pandemic regulations. Detective Inspector Stamper took great pains to point out that the camping trip had been right at the beginning of the COVID-19 restrictions, when rules were changing rapidly. He understood that people may be frightened that they had been in violation of the restrictions, which carried hefty penalties, but reassured anyone who came forward with any information that they would not get in trouble.

He finished with a plea: "If anyone has any information, however, insignificant they may feel it is—there may be background information or sightings, anything— please contact Crime Stoppers and provide that information."

Both families released public statements on the same day.

A family spokesperson on behalf of Russell Hill said: "We are deeply saddened that Russell and Carol have been missing for one month now. Russell is our brother, husband, dad and pa and Carol has been a friend of the family for a long time. The police, SES and volunteers have searched extensively, and we thank them whole-heartedly. It is devastating for our family that we don't know what has happened to them both. We are pleading for anyone who has any information to please come forward."

A family spokesperson on behalf of Carol Clay said: "Carol Clay and Russell Hill have been missing in the Wonnangatta Valley area in Victoria since 20 March 2020. Carol's family is very shocked and worried by their disappearance and ask for information from the community. We appeal to anyone who may have been in the area at the same time who may have seen Carol and Russell, their campsite or vehicle. Anyone who has any knowledge at all of their whereabouts could they please contact the police. Their disappearance is very out of character as they were well prepared and travelling in country which was well known to Russell Hill. This is a very difficult time for our family. We are living with uncertainty, loss, and the continual stress of not knowing where they are and what has happened. At this time we ask that our privacy be fully respected while we deal as a family with the ongoing process of supporting each other, dealing with the issues this raises and helping the police. We would also very much like to take this opportunity to extend our thanks and gratitude to the many people who have taken part in the search in difficult terrain and those who are continuing to work hard to solve what is at this stage an absolute mystery."

Internet sleuths dissected the statements and clues, and social media soon became an online frenzy of theories and conjecture about what could possibly have happened to Russell and Carol.

LOST CAMPERS

"There are parts of this bushland that have probably never been walked on by humans. It is that remote."
– Tony Combridge, Detective Acting Inspector, Missing Persons Squad

Although the physical search was called off as Victoria entered winter, a time when the area became even less accessible than usual, police maintained an active investigation. In late May, they announced they were looking into three potential sightings of the couple on March 22, a day after the first hikers found the burned-out campsite. Detectives asked to speak to anyone who had been near Howitt Plains and Zeka Spur Track on March 19 or March 20, or the Wonnangatta Valley and Wonnangatta Station between March 20 and March 24.

As the mystery of the vanished pair deepened, it captured the imagination of the nation. Everyone had a theory about what had become of the elderly couple.

The police, if not some of the press commentators, had completely discounted the theory that the pair had staged their own deaths to start a new life together. One of Carol Clay's close friends, Dorothy Coombe, told the Australian TV show *A Current Affair* that the grandmother "loved and adored" her family and wanted to see her grandkids grow up.

Police also ruled out a possible murder-suicide. The more fanciful commentators on the stories that periodically appeared in the press and on social media came up with far-fetched theories, such as that people who disapproved of the affair had sent a hitman after them. This was a notion so ridiculous that police gave it no airtime at all.

However, as well as ruling out theories more at home on a daytime soap opera, they were also beginning to discount the original and most likely scenario: that Russell and Carol had simply gotten lost.

There was much to lend credence to this idea. All around the area, where walking paths branch off the main tracks, signs warn walkers that they are entering dangerous and challenging terrain, where water can be difficult or impossible to find and only the most experienced, physically fit, and well-equipped walkers should attempt to navigate through the bush.

Both the drone and controller were missing and Russell was still learning the ropes of his sophisticated, but temperamental, new toy. According to the Australian TV program *Under Investigation*, a nearby camper claimed that Russell had flown his drone over the other man's campsite on the evening of Friday (which the man called "disrespectful"). Given that the couple didn't start setting up until after 6 p.m., that would have been bordering on dark. Russell may have been hoping to capture sunset footage of the magnificent Piemans Falls and Bryce Gorge area nearby. Could Russell and Carol have gone looking for a lost drone and gotten lost themselves?

The DJI Mavic 2 is a portable hobbyist drone that folds away to fit into a rucksack, or even fanny pack, easily. Like most drones, it has a frustratingly short battery life, but is sophisticated enough that it will return to base if the operator presses the button, if it flies out of range, or if the battery is running low. This function is said to be reliable. It also has collision avoidance so, theoretically, it shouldn't crash into a tree or rock. However, some critics claim that the Mavic 2 is also prone to rare random fly-away events and might "bug out" occasionally. In the hands of an inexperienced pilot, there are many scenarios where an error of judgment could risk losing the drone.

If Russell had tried to retrieve the drone from somewhere inaccessible, he may have fallen or otherwise hurt himself. He had a heart condition, which may have been exacerbated by the exertion of looking for the drone. If Carol had been with him, she may not have been equipped to handle an emergency. It was Russell who was experienced in the ways of the bush. If Carol had gone to look for help, she could easily have gotten lost herself.

Alternatively, if she had been left behind and Russell called out for help, she may have tried to find him. As an inexperienced camper, Carol may have left the stove on, causing the fire which obliterated their tent and belongings.

In the depths of the High Country, there is a very real

risk of dying quickly from exposure or dehydration due
to the harsh elements. There is a large population of wild
dogs in the area that an injured or lost/dying person
could easily fall prey to.

The theory of the two becoming lost and falling
victims to wild dogs, which would soon pick apart their
carcasses, was the most obvious and the most plausible
reason for a pair of campers to go missing. However, if
this was the case, at least some sign of them, their
clothing or their belongings would surely have been
found after the extensive explorations of the area, which
included hunting by cadaver dogs, aerial searches, highly
experienced teams of local bushmen and professional
search and rescue squads. It was also noted that there
were a large number of deer carcasses in the area that
had not been touched by wild dogs, which would usually
go for the easiest pickings first.

Fire forensics expert Greg Kelly told *Under Investigation* that he had experimented with the tent and ropes
materials to see if a fire could have started accidentally. In
each experiment, the fibers caught fire but burned slowly
and very quickly extinguished themselves before a blaze
properly ignited. In order to create the inferno that
destroyed the camp, he felt a deliberate accelerant would
have been needed. The fire was unlikely to be caused by
an unattended camp stove.

The three most straightforward theories—elopement,
suicide pact and getting lost—had dropped down the
investigators' list. As time went on, police became
increasingly convinced that they were looking for
another person or persons in relation to Russell and
Carol's disappearance.

THEORIES AND SUPPOSITION

"The most likely scenario is that there are others involved in this."
– Tony Combridge, Detective Acting Inspector, Missing Persons Squad

One of the first things detectives considered was that Russell and Carol had stumbled onto a drug crop, or more likely, the drone had flown over one and taken photographs that certain people might object to. The area is known to be home to illegal marijuana crops, which can be easily camouflaged in the dense scrub, and the timing of their disappearance broadly coincided with the end-of-summer harvest time.

It was possible that Russell and Carol were murdered at their campsite and their bodies taken to another location, or that they were taken away to be executed elsewhere. All their belongings that had photo capabilities (the drone and their phones) were taken and then the campsite had been set alight—perhaps to cover the killers' tracks and destroy any DNA that had been left behind.

However, most of these illegal crops are in more accessible areas than where Russell and Carol were camped, and they are generally of just a few hundred plants—hardly on the scale of organized crime. For large-scale operations, bush crops have mostly been replaced by greenhouse crops. No significant operations were spotted by any of the ground or aerial search teams. There are any number of more convenient and accessible areas in which to grow a bush crop and, if there had been one out there, police would have found it.

Detective Inspector Andrew Stamper told reporters after many extensive searches, "We're pretty certain there's no drug crop activity involved in this investigation."

However, Detective Inspector Stamper told *A Current Affair* that investigators did believe that someone else was involved and the most compelling theory was that "something bad has happened to them and they've either been removed from the valley or they've been concealed somewhere."

It may have been something as simple as a campers' altercation. Russell was not the kind of man to back down from an argument or to stay silent if someone annoyed him or was doing something he believed to be wrong or disrespectful. Alternatively, it could have been Russell who annoyed other campers by flying his drone above their campsite. Drones are a particularly polarizing piece of equipment in remote camp areas, and many people resent their intrusive noise and camera. Few remote campers want a drone hovering over their secluded site.

It was plausible that such an argument could have turned violent. At 74, and with a heart condition, Russell was a prime candidate to be killed by a single punch by a younger man. If the man panicked, he may have also killed Carol and then burned the campsite to cover his tracks, taking the couple's bodies to be disposed of elsewhere.

It was unlikely an attack on the couple was "planned" or "premeditated," Inspector Stamper told *A Current Affair*. "The strongest theory is that it is something that's happened in the valley that has escalated and resulted in something bad happening to them."

HILL PEOPLE AND THE BUTTON MAN

"They say no one knows he is near until he decides to make himself known. A wildlife photographer spent days taking shots in the area near the Button Man's camp. When he returned home and downloaded his photos to his computer there was one unexplained shot of the photographer asleep inside his tent. No one knows who took the shot."
– John Silvester, "The Button Man Could be key to mounting mountain mystery," *The Age, May 22, 2020*

Among the locals in the nearby town of Mansfield and surrounds, there are persistent rumors about "hill people." These are folk who originally worked as miners in the area, set themselves up in extremely remote and isolated houses, and then simply never returned to society after the mines closed. Supposedly, some live in communities and some live alone. Very occasionally, one will venture into town and buy up months of supplies.

One of the most well-known of the mythical hill

people is the Button Man. He got his nickname thanks to his hobby of making buttons out of bones and the antlers of deer hunted in the region. This is an old and well-respected craft, but when paired with other stories, it becomes something more ominous.

A few months after Russell and Carol's disappearance, several news articles appeared that conflated stories of the large number of unsolved deaths and disappearances in the area with the mysterious Button Man. Although not directly stated, the implication was that the Button Man might have, if not direct involvement in some or all of the incidents, then at least some knowledge of what happened.

The last confirmed sighting of missing hiker Niels Becker had been by the Button Man, who told police he saw the well-equipped hiker in his area. The track took him past the Button Man's camp.

The Button Man was described as an elderly, but fit and wiry, man who was heavily tattooed and wore over-sized earplugs fashioned from bone that extended his lobes almost to his shoulders. He had turned his back on society many years earlier, living on the land in the High Country. He reportedly set up one of his camps on the side of a remote mountain, which let him see anyone who was approaching, and counted cars by making a pyramid of rocks. He was described as an expert bushman and a loner, who didn't like strangers encroaching on the land he had claimed as his own. His home camp was located deep in the wilderness, well away from the public camp-sites, and he lived alone, a hermit-like existence.

There were many stories of him chasing away campers or hikers who came too close to his site and acting in a decidedly odd, if not overtly violent, manner. He would pepper interlopers with rapid-fire questions, and would ask solo campers or hikers if they were alone and if anyone knew where they were. They told stories of him arriving to their campfires out of the darkness and sitting down uninvited, before outstaying his welcome with his unnerving ways and grim conversation topics. He would grill the intruders about why they were there, but would never answer questions about himself. Sometimes he would ask if they wanted to see his ax collection, an offer few were brave enough to take him up on.

Locals who stashed firewood supplies in hidden crevices had their stockpiles raided under cover of night. One experienced camper reported going to bed and rising the next morning to discover the Button Man had erected a tent right next to his head in complete silence as he slept. And then there was the photographer who reported the unexplained photograph of him sleeping, which he discovered only when he was looking through his pictures later.

Another story involved a group of scouts on an overnight trip on the Bogong High Plains. One scout had brought a guitar for a singalong, but when the guitar needed tuning, they stopped and retired for the night. They awoke to find their guitar perfectly tuned and a single set of ski trails heading off into the distance.

With such creepy campfire tales in no short supply, newspapers were enamored by the mystique of the Button Man. Articles soon appeared that fell just short of implicating him in the disappearances in the area over the years. The *Daily Mail* described him as "spooky," "ominous" and "bloody scary." But tales about the Button

Man were always vague or secondhand. The photographer's story in particular seems to be a rehash of old urban legends.

However, Mansfield locals were quick to come to his defense, painting a picture of a cantankerous but innocent man who just wanted to be left alone in his advancing years. They said he visited the town often for supplies and was generally friendly and—although somewhat eccentric—could hold an intelligent conversation. He gratefully accepted canned goods from local hunters to help him through the winter. All the local bushmen knew him and admired his skills and local knowledge. There was no doubt he had his finger on the pulse of who was camping where, but he was just a person who liked to keep to himself.

Rhyll McCormack, a journalist at the *Mansfield Courier*, broke ranks with the mainstream press when she wrote a scathing indictment on the media outlets who were happy to bend the truth for the sake of a story. "The 'Button Man' of Mansfield has been tried, found guilty and hung out to dry by metro media outlets across the country," she wrote. "What is certain is that the 70-year-old Button Man will no longer feel welcome in Mansfield anytime soon. That seeking solace from society has made him a target of suspicion, regardless of whether he deserved it or not."

With so much scrutiny on the Button Man, police felt compelled to question him. They came away convinced of what they had already suspected: there was nothing to indicate the mysterious loner had killed the couple, or anyone else in the High Country. He was more likely to be a source of useful information than a suspect in their case.

However, the damage had been done. The Button Man had become the last thing in the world he would have wanted to be: a tourist attraction. Some news reports had pinpointed the area of his camp and even provided handy maps. Curious townies started driving out there with the sole purpose of spotting the Button Man and taking photographs of the recluse who just wanted to be left alone.

Later reports tell of the Button Man being hassled and his camp ransacked after the news stories. He had to be taken to a safe house until strangers stopped seeking him out. Rhyll McCormack told SBS News: "The so-called button man is as local to Mansfield as you are going to get. He was not a pariah in Mansfield, the way he was made out to be down in Melbourne." She said that a TV crew tried to employ her to take them to his camp, unannounced, so that they could interview him, which she refused to do.

The legend of the Button Man grew to be an urban myth of its own. The media created a bogeyman that distracted from the fact that two elderly people were still missing and there were no clues about what may have happened to them.

HUNTING MISHAPS

As time wore on with no sign of the elderly pair, a new theory emerged as the dominant one favored by police. They believed that there had been a mishap involving hunters. This theory was bolstered when the second camper to come across the burned-out campsite recalled finding a fluorescent green crossbow arrow nearby. It was not an unusual sight, so he didn't think much of it at the time, but brought it up when the Missing Persons Squad pleaded for any information, no matter how insignificant it might seem.

Deer are plentiful in the High Country, and deer hunters were known to illegally hunt in the area. Sambar deer are the most common species in Victoria, and it is legal to hunt them all year round by those with the correct license, providing they use approved methods. Sambar deer antlers are prized by hunters as trophies because of their size and the ability of the deer to evade people. Fresh-killed deer heads can sell for high prices. Hunting by stalking is legal all year round. Illegal hunters use spotlights, causing the deer to freeze in the light and making them easy targets. There are strict rules concerning hunting in certain places—such as around campsites, along the sides of the road and near homes.

It is illegal to spotlight deer or to use dogs for most of the year. According to a representative of the Sporting Shooters Association of Australia, "Such behaviour is condemned by all ethical hunters and such individuals are not looked kindly upon. However, such behaviour is not necessarily premeditated or motivated by criminal intent. Some individuals act illegally simply through ignorance of relevant legislation."

Those who knew Russell well believed that he would not have shied away from a confrontation. He was the type of guy, they said, who didn't take crap from anyone. If, for instance, Russell's drone had spied some illegal hunting, while he may not have confronted the hunters or even turned them in, as it wasn't any of his business, if they demanded he hand over his drone, he most certainly would have stood his ground. He may have been accidentally killed in any ensuing altercation, and then Carol subsequently murdered to get rid of any witnesses.

Alternatively, locals believe that either Russell or Carol may have been accidentally shot by hunters with a crossbow or rifle after being mistaken for prey. The thermal imaging that hunters use on their high-powered rifles does not return a clear image, and if they were not expecting campers to be nearby, a person could easily be mistaken for one of the large bucks that roam the hills. Realizing their mistake, and knowing that they could be charged with negligent homicide, the hunter or hunters could have killed the other person in a panic and disposed of their bodies deep in the bush, where the wild dogs would take care of the rest.

High Country musterer Lachlan Culican, who helped police during the search, told *Under Investigation* that he came across an unusual number of slaughtered deer with their antlers cut off in the area when he was searching for the couple. He said he saw a new carcass every 700 or 800 feet, which suggested a high number of illegal hunters in the area. Although there is no legal requirement to remove deer carcasses from the bush, ethical hunters try to ensure as much of the animal is used as possible. While the antlers are the most prized part of the kill, venison is a high-protein, high-iron and low-fat meat that many people enjoy eating.

Detectives posited a theory that the killers may have bundled the pair up in their sleeping bags to move them to another location and then torched the campsite to destroy forensic evidence of a crime.

A representative of the Sporting Shooters Association said, "There is significant concern that career criminals are now conducting illegal poaching on an organised, or semi-organised, basis and are selling antlers to fund drug activity. As an Association this is particularly concerning because these people are labelled as 'hunters,' when they are in fact nothing more than criminals carrying out illegal activity. They are not hunting, and are certainly not considered to be 'hunters' by any true hunter. Unfortunately there is no particularly appropriate term for these people that differentiates them from real hunters, or at least not one that the media use to make a distinction."

AN OPEN INVESTIGATION

A year passed, and with no sign of the couple, the prognosis was grim. Police had all but ruled out the theories that they had gotten lost or had an accident, confirming that they believed the couple to be dead and the victims of foul play. There was a brief window of optimism that a break in the case was imminent in March 2021, when a drone was found in the area and handed into police. It was reported to be an identical model to Russell's, but within days police determined that it had not belonged to the missing man. Also in March, with interest in the missing persons case revitalized, police appealed to the public for information about a "mystery vehicle"—a white utility truck that was the only vehicle in the area that had not been identified. Police cadaver dogs were again brought in to search for the missing Victorian campers but found nothing of note.

In April 2021, acting on unspecified information, investigators suddenly moved their investigation to Great Alpine Road in Mount Hotham area, 50 miles to the north-west of the burned-out campsite. During a search in a small area of bushland, they retrieved two shovels, which were bagged and entered into evidence. The shovels were not suitable for digging holes in the ground large enough to bury a body, but were designed for moving loose fill, like wet concrete or sand or snow. Police were tightlipped about whether there was any significance to the shovels and did not share any theories with the media.

Soon after discovering the shovels, police moved the search back to Wonnangatta, "as a result of information obtained from previous searches." Their efforts were focused on the Dargo High Plains Road, Cynthia Range Track, Herne Spur Track, and the Wonnangatta Track. Detective Acting Inspector Tony Combridge told a press conference that while there were no suspects, there were "several persons of interest."

"I think that the most likely scenario is still the scenario that there are other parties involved in this," he said.

In May, Russell's wife spoke to *The Australian* newspaper, saying that, although she believed her husband to be dead, she hoped that the two of them would be found and have to come home to "face the music." She admitted this was unlikely, as Russell had not accessed any of his bank accounts and there had been no other indications that he might still be alive.

The Country Women's Association apparently did not approve of the publicity surrounding their former President's ostensible illicit affair with a married man and quietly removed Carol's name as one of only six CWA members of honor from the CWA newsletter.

Local historian Keith Laydon told *The Age* on May 30, 2021, "I don't think the police are looking for a person in the latest case. I think they're looking for evidence. And I think they know who it was."

Since then, while the investigation remains very much open, there has been no further information about the missing campers. Mystery still surrounds the disappearance of Russell Hill and Carol Clay.

BLUE SKIES, BLACK DEATH

WHAT HAPPENED TO STEPHEN HILDER?

INTRODUCTION

Accidents are to be expected in skydiving. It is, after all, an extreme sport. Over ninety-nine per cent of people who jump out of an airplane will do it just once, attached to an instructor. Those people are unlikely to come to any harm, as they are hooked onto somebody who has done thousands of jumps and who makes all the decisions for them. They will mark a tick on their bucket list and never do it again.

For that tiny fraction who go on to jump solo, skydiving becomes more than a thrill. It is an obsession, a lifestyle, something they *are* rather than merely something they do. Those just starting out are bound to experience scrapes and bruises, perhaps even a broken bone or two, as they get used to the elements of the sport—freefall, canopy flight and landing. Deaths are rare, but most skydivers are prepared to encounter a fatal accident at some time during their jumping career if they stick with the sport for long enough. There is a universal traditional toast for when a jumper loses his or her life: *Blue Skies, Black Death*.

Accidents are to be expected in skydiving, but skydivers do what they can to minimize the risks to themselves and others. They check their own gear and that of the people they are jumping with, looking for anything amiss—frayed loops that may not hold a closing pin in properly, flaps that have become untucked, webbing that is wearing out. They make sure that everyone who has taken off in the plane has landed safely and returned to the hangar. Like many groups of people in high-risk, high-tension environments, they become close-knit, often exclusionary of outsiders.

Skydivers look out for each other. Nobody locks their car, and they routinely leave bags and wallets carelessly out in the open, their owners confident they will still be there when they come back. The community is built on adrenaline and trust. But in the summer of 2003, that trust among skydivers was broken in a most shocking way at a drop zone in Lancashire, UK. The phrase *Blue Skies, Black Death* took on a sinister new meaning.

Accidents are to be expected in skydiving. But nobody expects murder.

MONDAY, JUNE 30

Q: Why do you want to jump out of a perfectly good
airplane?
A: There's no such thing as a *perfectly good* airplane

Twenty-year-old Stephen Hilder spent Monday, June 30, 2003, at a theme park with his girl-friend, Ruth Woodhouse. The two enjoyed a casual day together before parting to head in different directions—Ruth heading home to the south and Stephen embarking on a 100-mile drive north, to the parachuting drop zone at Hibaldstow Airfield, in Lincolnshire, UK.

Stephen was embarking on what he hoped would be a solid week of skydiving. Ruth often joked that he got withdrawal symptoms if he hadn't jumped for a few days. He had become obsessed with the sport, to the point of missing an exam in favor of going jumping and maxing out his credit cards to buy the expensive equipment involved. He jumped as often as possible, traveling to other parts of the world when the weather in Britain became too cold. Ruth had taken her first jump three weeks before, with the enthusiastic support of Stephen, but she was not yet sure that the sport was for her.

Stephen hadn't been able to jump on Saturday because he had spent the day at a Bon Jovi concert in Hyde Park. He had taken his father to the concert as an early birthday present, though it was hard to say whether the gift was more for his dad or for himself. He had managed to get in a couple of jumps at his home drop zone, Netheravon, on the Sunday before spending the day with Ruth on Monday.

Stephen made the long drive instead of going to his usual drop zone because Hibaldstow was hosting the collegiate nationals, a competition between college skydiving clubs. Stephen was a first-year engineering student and officer cadet at the Royal Military College of Science at Shrivenham, Wiltshire. At around 300 jumps, Stephen was considered an intermediate-level skydiver and would be jumping in a three-man team with two friends who were at a similar stage of parachuting experience. His teammates were on a military course and would not be able to get there until later in the week, but Stephen hoped to get a few jumps in before they arrived.

As he turned into the driveway of the airfield with a variety of hangars and buildings dotted around, Stephen probably felt like he was coming home. Many drop zones cater solely to tandem students. One-time thrill seekers provide a quick and easy profit for drop zone operators and a steady income for instructors, parachute packers and office staff at airfields. Although Hibaldstow did offer tandem skydives, it was known as being a place that was run by skydivers for skydivers, which made it particularly popular with experienced jumpers.

As well as the office, there were team training rooms where teams could review their jumps on video. Anyone could grab one of the available "creepers" that were provided—body boards on castor wheels. Skydivers lay flat on their stomachs and whizzed around the concrete floor of the hangar to practice the formations they later hoped to achieve in the sky. A bar and lounge area was a welcoming space for après-jump socializing and the occasional wild party. It was where many adrenaline junkies found their tribe.

There were bunkrooms where jumpers could hire a bed at the drop zone if they wanted to, but few skydivers did that. They preferred to pitch tents, throw down a mattress in the corner of a hangar, or sleep in their cars, as Stephen did. The money they saved could be better spent on jumps.

It was a quiet night when he arrived, and Stephen retired after a couple of drinks at the drop zone bar. There would be plenty of time to party later in the week.

TUESDAY, JULY 1 – WEDNESDAY, JULY 2

The weather was threatening to be unkind to skydivers that week. No planes took off at all on Tuesday, and chief instructor Paul Hollow soon announced that jumping was off for the day. Once the official announcement was made, the skydivers were free to leave the drop zone or start drinking. Stephen drove eleven miles to a gas station, where he bought some junk food.

On Wednesday, there were just two or three plane-loads before the skydivers were once again grounded. Stephen was on one of these, doing a jump with a coach who was wearing a camera on his helmet so that when Stephen's teammates arrived later that evening, they could critique his style. Nobody knows whether he packed his parachute himself after landing or hired one of the professional packers to do it for him, but it was likely to be the former. Most skydivers pack their main parachutes themselves, but there is always someone else ready to do it for beer money. Stephen usually packed his own after a jump.

Stephen left his packed parachute in the kit room—a room where the walls were lined with racks for hanging parachutes on by their shoulder straps, keeping them off the ground. Hanging the parachutes up neatly in rows made it easy for a skydiver to identify and grab his or her kit when it was time for a jump. This room was typically not monitored. It was open to anybody on the drop zone to come and go as they please. The kit room at Hibaldstow also doubled as a lounge room, where skydivers could hang out or watch TV when not jumping.

Stephen Hilder's teammates arrived that evening. Adrian Blair and David Mason, both nineteen years old, were cadets with Stephen at the military college. They had arrived just in time for the official competition welcome party in the drop zone bar. The trio drank, talked all things skydiving and joined in silly games like an adult version of "pass the parcel." Most of the seventy-eight competitors had arrived by that time and they hoped that the contest would be starting on Thursday. Everyone wanted to be at peak performance, so by drop zone standards, the party was quiet and ended reasonably early.

Stephen and his teammates retired to get a good night's sleep before the competition started the next day.

THURSDAY, JULY 3

Unfortunately, the weather had other plans. Thunderstorms lashed much of the UK, which was experiencing a heatwave. Skydivers were advised early that there would be no jumping that day, and quite likely none the next day either.

With skydiving not an option, the competitors, drop zone staff and other skydivers—known as "fun jumpers" —had to find something else to do. Stephen Hilder went shopping to find something to wear for the fancy-dress party that was to be held that evening, while his teammates went to the cinema. In the great college tradition, a scavenger hunt was organized in the afternoon, with porn and female underwear on the list of items competitors had to come up with, and bonus points for completing random gross tasks. Stephen valiantly scoffed down some dog food in an effort to win the prize, although the prize was so inconsequential that, afterwards, nobody could remember what it was.

After a barbecue dinner, the three teammates spent a

couple of hours getting ready before moving on to the drop zone bar around 9 p.m. The party was already in full swing, with many people having started drinking in the early afternoon. The oppressive heat inside the shed where the bar was housed ensured everyone was thirsty.

The theme of the fancy-dress party that evening was to come dressed as any character starting with the letters B, C, P, or A, the acronym of the British Collegiate Parachute Association, the organizers of the event. The truly lazy would turn up dressed in their jumpsuits as "parachutists," but many made more of an effort. Among the cops, cheerleaders, punks, pilots, and angels, several of the male contestants dressed in drag, declaring they had come as "bitches." Stephen Hilder, wearing a leather dress he had found at a thrift store earlier that day, was one of them.

Skydivers are known to party hard at the best of times, but a bunch of college-aged competitors who have the pent-up frustration of not having jumped and the likelihood of not being able to jump the next day, can take it to the extreme. The bar did a roaring trade that night.

Nobody was surprised when Stephen grabbed the karaoke microphone to belt out some Bon Jovi tunes. He was a natural performer, whose other hobby was amateur dramatics, which was how he met Ruth. If it weren't for rehearsals for the college play, he and Ruth would rarely see each other, as Stephen spent every weekend jumping out of planes. Tonight, he sang deliberately terribly, to the delight of the crowd, hideous in his make-up and skimpy leather dress paired with trainers. With the confidence borne of copious amounts of Red Bull and vodka, Steve,

Adrian, and David could be found at various times of the night howling progressively cheesier tunes into the microphone together.

The party broke up at 2:30 a.m. There was still the chance of competition jumps the next day if the weather cleared and there is a strict rule that skydivers and pilots alike must adhere to: "eight hours between bottle and throttle". When weather permits, jumping starts soon after sunrise, and if a safety officer had seen a skydiver drinking at 2 a.m., they would not be allowed to board a plane until at least 10 a.m., which in competition could mean forfeiting a round and scoring a zero.

People's memories were hazy after the party. There may or may not have been arguments or fights. Stephen may or may not have been involved in them. It depended on who you asked and how much they'd had to drink that night. Some skydivers got so drunk they could not recall anything that happened that evening or the early hours of the next morning to themselves, let alone anyone else.

FRIDAY, JULY 4

S tephen Hilder slept late the next morning, as did a good number of people at the drop zone, knowing that once they started moving, the hang-overs would kick in. There was no hurry to get up, as the day was overcast and parachuting through cloud was considered dangerous and, in most cases, prohibited.

After emerging from his car, where he had spent the night, Stephen joined a game of cards in the drop zone cafe as competitors waited for chief instructor, Paul Hollow, to give the all-clear to jump. It was touch and go, but finally, the competitors were told that if the break in the weather held on, they could jump after lunch.

Stephen, Adrian, and David were more than ready to be on the first load of the day. They were excited for this competition, as their team, "Black Rain," was doing well. Earlier that year, they had come third in one regional competition and then won another. The lads grabbed their gear from the kit room. This was a job that could be done on autopilot, as each skydiver's parachute harness is distinctive. Stephen's was black, white, and gray; unusual in its lack of brighter colors.

The first step was to turn on the tiny electronic device —known as a Cypres—that would release the reserve parachute if its owner was still in freefall at 1,200 feet, far lower than they should be. If a skydiver had not released their parachute by then, they were only around six seconds from impact with the ground.

Most skydivers had a Cypres, although nobody ever admitted it was because they might become distracted and forget to deploy. Most claimed to have the life-saving device only in the rare case they got knocked out or somehow incapacitated in freefall. In that case, the Cypres would fire, cutting through the loop that holds in the spring-loaded reserve pilot chute, giving the skydiver the best chance of landing safely, even if they were unconscious.

Once the little screen confirmed that the Cypres was activated, Stephen gave his gear a quick check to ensure nothing looked amiss—no flaps untucked, or frayed closing loops and to check that the pilot chute was snugly tucked in its sleeve. The pilot chute is a miniature parachute that sits in an elastic sleeve at the bottom of the container, with just a padded cushion sticking out. When it is time to deploy, the skydiver grabs hold of the pad and pulls the pilot chute out. Once it hits the air, it inflates, pulling the pin that allows the main parachute out of the container. If the pilot chute is not packed in securely on takeoff, it can be knocked out of its pocket prematurely. At best, this would mean a very long, cold, and lonely canopy flight to the ground. At worst, it could become wrapped around a limb and result in disaster.

The team then donned their jumpsuits and parachutes and performed a "dirt dive," a ritualistic dance mimicking the formations they had to do in the sky. Each new formation earned them a point. The lads laughed and ribbed each other and hammed it up for their cameraman, someone drawn from the competition's camera pool and whom they didn't know particularly well. The cameraman's job was to fly a little above the team and make sure every point was captured so that it could be judged.

Some people considered Stephen a little cocky, but that was par for the course for young men involved in extreme sports, especially when they were doing well. Barely out of his teens, Stephen had the bulletproof shield only youth and testosterone can provide. Older skydivers are well aware of the problems that come with cockiness arising from a skill level that exceeds jump numbers but does not have the benefit of experience. They make sure that the young jumpers don't forget their safety checks. The highest-risk group for serious injury is young males with around 200 to 500 jumps, jumping with a fast, high-performance parachute.

All three of the Black Rain lads had pumped out jumps at a much faster rate than average. Adrian and Dave were particularly close and had been through their initial training together the previous December. Since then, virtually all of their skydives had been together, many of them in the US, where planes were bigger, drop zones busier, and jumping was a year-round sport.

Communication between the young blokes was usually lighthearted and centered around the sport, but sometimes their conversations went a little deeper. Just the week before, Adrian had posed the philosophical question: *do you want to live forever?* Dave countered, tongue in cheek: "You seem to imply that we're gonna die? I thought that we were all young and invincible ... gonna live forever no matter what sorta stupid things we do."

Adrian responded: "I don't wanna die—but I'm not scared of it. The way I see it is that if I died now I'd have died happy. I wanna try everything there is to do—then find some more stuff that nobody has thought of doing yet. And if I don't make it all the way? Well hey—I want my friends to carry on having a kick ass time. Blue skies forever."

Stephen was not part of that conversation, but previously the three had talked about different ways of dying. Stephen had claimed if he was going to commit suicide, he would want to jump out of a plane. The other two agreed it would be better than dying in a road accident or by shooting yourself. Such morbid conversations were not unusual among skydivers. They often go hand-in-hand with the black humor unique to extreme sports.

What is the difference between a bad golfer and a bad skydiver?
A bad golfer goes, WHACK, "SHIT."
A bad skydiver goes, "SHIT," WHACK.

For all their larrikin behavior, Stephen's Black Rain team took safety seriously, but especially so Stephen. In fact, Adrian and David, who had done many of their jumps in the US, where there is a stronger emphasis on personal responsibility and less on rules and regulations, often found Steve's rigid adherence to the British Para-chute Association's safety manual annoying. Sometimes they would play pranks on the older cadet, like booking him in for a student jump that he was overqualified for, or hiding pieces of his gear. The pranks were designed to annoy, rather than be dangerous.

Just prior to boarding the plane, the three men performed a flightline check on each other, once again making sure that everything was as it should be. Stephen performed the check on both his teammates, and Dave performed the check on Stephen, each patting the back-pack of the other firmly once they had finished, code for "You're good to go." Dave had developed a pattern that covered all points in a methodical order, which he stuck to every time. He believed that if you changed your system, it was too easy to miss something that was not as it should be.

One other team shared the plane, making a total of eight skydivers on board the Technoavia SM92 Finist aircraft. Drop zone planes have no seats, so the skydivers sat on the floor, facing the rear, each person sitting between the legs of the skydiver behind them. The two cameramen knelt at the back of the plane, facing forward so they could see everyone on board. The propeller fired up for the first load of the day and Black Rain's first jump for the competition.

As the plane climbed with its eight skydivers on board, Black Rain's videographer turned on his camera. The footage would later show Stephen Hilder laughing and joking. As the plane got near to the competition height of 13,000 feet, he and his teammates did one last gear check. They performed a ritual handshake before climbing into position in the door of the airplane.

The three launched off the edge of the door to the sky, their cameraman above them. Their exit didn't go completely to plan—it "funneled" in skydiver-speak, meaning they didn't come off cleanly—but they recovered after a few seconds and started their maneuvers. After ten seconds, the skydivers would have reached terminal velocity, the speed at which the body stops accelerating. At this stage, the jumper is falling at around 120 mph, or 200 kph, toward the earth. For the next forty-five seconds, the team continually changed their hand and leg grips, creating a new formation, or point, each time.

For an intermediate team, 10 points is good, and 15 points is excellent. That day, Black Rain turned a competition-leading 19 points. It was the best jump the team had ever done together, and they knew it before their freefall was even finished. Barring a miracle from another team, they would be crowned national champions. The three exhilarated men made eye contact and screamed through their huge grins at each other, although it was impossible to hear anything through the wind rushing up and past the ears. It was enough to see each other's elated smiles and tongues sticking out as they celebrated a job well done.

At 4,000 feet, around a minute after they exited the plane, the three teammates turned away from each other to gain horizontal separation before they deployed their parachutes. At that stage, the camera no longer needed to keep filming, but in any case, the cameraman lost sight of them due to cloud.

The first thing skydivers are trained to do after deploying their parachutes is to look around to see where everyone else is in the sky. Two people colliding in midair spells disaster, as their parachutes could become entangled, resulting in a double fatality. Nobody saw Stephen's purple parachute that day, but Adrian Blair remembered seeing a big wad of white fabric. It registered as out of place, but he was thinking about the amazing jump he'd just done and the landing—usually the most dangerous part of the skydive—was coming up. The sensory overload meant he didn't make anything of it at the time.

Chief instructor Paul Hollow was on the ground, making sure as many people who went up in the plane returned to the hangar. Especially with the cloudy weather, it would not be unusual for a skydiver to land in the cornfields, which were almost at harvest time and taller than an average person, requiring a rescue mission. Anyone making such a transgression would have to buy a case of beer that night and ring a bell hung above the bar for just such an occasion, alerting the thirsty hoards that there was free alcohol to be had and an errant skydiver to be made fun of.

It looked like there would be free beer today. Paul Hollow dispatched one of his instructors to go and pick up what he thought was a skydiver who had landed under their white reserve parachute way past the landing area. The drop zone chief tried to ignore the uneasy feeling that something hadn't been quite right about the off-drop zone landing.

When the confused instructor came back with a

bundle in his arms, Paul Hollow's years of experience meant he only had to glance at the parachute to know he was now looking for a body. The material was white, the color of a reserve parachute. A main parachute may be many colors, but only reserve parachutes are white. The fact that this reserve parachute was not attached to a person could only mean one thing.

Although accidents are accepted as being an integral part of skydiving, deaths are rare, and death by double malfunction—where both parachutes fail—are almost unheard of. Usually, some sort of error on the part of the skydiver causes a fatality. They may turn their parachute too close to the ground, hoping to build up speed for a really cool landing, but misjudge and hit too hard. They may deal badly with a malfunction of their main parachute and deploy their reserve parachute into it, causing the two to tangle. Two skydivers might collide—either in freefall or under their parachutes—rendering one or both unconscious and unable to land safely.

Although a double malfunction is rare, but not unheard of, Paul Hollow had never seen or heard of an incident where a reserve parachute broke away from the rest of the skydiving kit and the person wearing it. Unlike a main parachute, which has special release rings so that a skydiver can jettison it if it is malfunctioning, a reserve parachute is permanently attached. There is no getting rid of it unless you physically cut it with a knife or climb out of the harness in midair.

Paul Hollow climbed onto the roof of the drop zone car and scanned the fields until he spotted a large indentation in the corn. This time, Hollow accompanied the instructor to the scene.

Stephen Hilder was lying on the ground, surrounded by the corn that had done nothing to break his fall as he hit the earth at almost 125 miles per hour. He was wearing his skydiving harness, but neither of his parachutes were billowing around him as would normally be expected. A single glance at Hilder's shoulder area told Paul Hollow all he needed to know. Stephen Hilder's parachute had been sabotaged. His gear had been tampered with.

Parachute sabotage is far more common in movies and TV than in real life, but it was not without precedent. Some cases did not result in anyone dying, either because it was discovered prior to the jump, or the sabotage was not absolute. However, in one case in Germany, a man who felt he had been friend-zoned by a fellow skydiver sabotaged her parachute, resulting in her death. The jealous would-be suitor was given life in prison for the murder.

The damage done to Stephen's kit could not be anything but deliberate and intended to kill. Hollow called the police.

WHEN DETECTIVE SUPERINTENDENT Colin Andrews of Humberside police arrived at the airfield, he knew he was dealing with a dead body. Local police were called as a matter of course if there was a death at the drop zone, and it usually involved a brief visit and a short report. However, when Paul Hollow took him aside and told him that the dead man's equipment had been interfered with, Andrews realized that this was no ordinary skydiving accident.

The local police were completely out of their depth when it came to the technicalities of the sport and its equipment, so they took the unusual step of calling in an independent skydiving expert to assist them with the investigation. John Hitchin from the British Parachute Association arrived to examine the scene to help determine what had happened to Stephen.

The skydiving experts quickly spotted what was wrong with the dead man's kit. Somebody had cut the long piece of webbing, called the bridle, that connects the pilot chute to the pin that opens the container where the main parachute is stored. The cut bridle and the pilot chute had been stuffed back into its elastic sleeve. There would have been no way of telling it was tampered with, without pulling the pilot chute out of its sleeve, and there would be no reason to do that unless something seemed suspicious or awry.

This meant that the pilot chute was no longer attached to the pin, so that when Stephen pulled it out at deployment height and let it go, there was nothing to pull the pin and drag the main canopy out of the container. Instead, the pin stayed lodged in there, and it would have been impossible for Stephen to do anything to get it out. Its location on top of the pack on his lower back was impossible to reach with bare hands.

Once he realized his main parachute was not coming out, Stephen pulled the handle that would deploy his white reserve canopy. This time, the parachute launched, but all four pieces of webbing (called the risers) that connected the canopy to the harness had been sliced through. With nothing attaching it to Stephen's kit, once the parachute hit the airstream, it simply flew away. To

Stephen, it would have looked like it vanished. He had no parachutes left and was still plummeting at terminal velocity.

All this would have happened between 4,000 and 2,000 feet above the ground. Stephen would have had at least ten to twenty seconds of knowing he was going to die and there was nothing he could do about it.

The Cypres he had so carefully set on the ground did its job, firing at 750 feet, but there was no reserve parachute for it to release. From the moment Stephen exited the aircraft, he was a dead man. Nothing could have saved him. What's more, whoever sabotaged his kit knew exactly what they were doing, both in terms of guaranteeing the sabotage would kill him, and ensuring it was done in such a manner that it would not be picked up by a regular preflight gear check. It could only have been somebody with intimate knowledge of skydiving equipment. It could only have been a skydiver.

The drop zone was officially declared a crime scene and everybody on the airfield—the seventy-eight competitors and twenty or so others—were asked not to leave until they had been spoken to by police. Detective Superintendent Andrews was sure that whoever killed Stephen Hilder was there and had watched him die.

A HUNDRED POTENTIAL MURDER
WEAPONS

P olice set to work interviewing everybody at the drop zone. Nobody was allowed to eat or drink until the insides of their cheeks could be swabbed for DNA. Every person on the airfield submitted to the DNA test willingly.

Not surprisingly, as soon as they were allowed to, all the skydivers carried out thorough checks of their own kits. The police insisted that everyone pop out their reserve parachutes—a big deal, as reserves are rarely deployed and have to be repacked by a certified reserve packer. Most skydivers are not qualified to pack their own and the professionals don't come cheap. The police wanted to determine whether Stephen had been targeted specifically, or if somebody had targeted random skydivers. There was no evidence that any other rig had been tampered with.

Police asked John Hitchin, the British Parachute Association expert, to cut some of Stephen's riser webbing so that it could be sent to a forensics laboratory for DNA testing. They provided Hitchin with kitchen scissors, which were loose and unable to cut through the thick material. Hitchin asked for a hook knife, which would easily slice through the webbing, being the job the knife was specifically designed for.

Hook knives, which are a standard part of a skydiver's kit, are knives that have a protected blade, are compact, easily stowed and removed, and attach to the harness. There are a couple of brands of knife that are specifically designed for skydiving use, and they are there as a last resort to cut through any equipment that has malfunctioned that could cause a hazard, for example, a parachute cord that is wrapped around a limb or helmet. Every skydiver carries one, which meant that the police had around a hundred potential murder weapons on the drop zone that day.

Another piece of evidence the police thought might shed some light on the events leading up to Stephen's death was video footage from the party the night before. Everyone who had taken any video or photographs of the party was asked to hand it over to police, who would later spend hours poring over every second, looking for something that might provide a clue.

Investigators asked everybody there if they could think of any motive for the murder, but they come up with nothing. It was not Stephen's usual drop zone, so he wasn't as well-known as the locals, but everyone who knew him or who had interacted with him that week claimed he was popular, fun-loving and an enthusiastic participant in everything, whether it was in the air, or the numerous activities skydivers keep themselves amused with on the ground when they are unable to jump. "He was a good lad, fun in the air and on the ground," said one friend.

The police had a time frame—the sabotage must have happened sometime between Stephen's last jump on Wednesday and the early hours of Friday morning—and a finite number of suspects. It had to be a skydiver who had been at the drop zone over those days, which came to less than 100 people. After many hours, the police left with over 200 pieces of potential evidence bagged and taken for testing. They were convinced the cuts must have been made with a hook knife, and they had DNA samples from everyone to compare against Stephen's equipment. It should not be long before a suspect was identified.

Less than forty-eight hours later, on Sunday, the skydivers, including Stephen's teammates Dave and Adrian, were back in the air, paying tribute to the young man who lost his life. However, all the skydivers had now added an extra step in their preflight checks. The sabotage had been expertly carried out to avoid detection during a preflight check. Now a firm tug on the reserve risers prior to jumping became part of the routine.

SEARCH FOR A MOTIVE

O ver the next week, police interviewed many people, including family, friends, skydivers who had been at the drop zone and Stephen's girlfriend, Ruth. They were hoping to find a motive—someone he had a beef with, jealousy or a perceived slight. The worst thing anyone could come up with was that Stephen could be arrogant. His mother described him as "an extraordinary son, an ordinary, infuriating lad who, above all else, loved skydiving."

Police reviewed every piece of footage from the party the night before, but all they found was a raucous celebration, where Stephen and his mates, looking ridiculous in their thrift-store dresses, sang equally ridiculous songs on the karaoke machine, cheered on by other partygoers. There was no sign of any tension, arguments, or fights. Indeed, any sort of aggression or violence was very rare at a drop zone and would have been noticed by those there.

The forensics lab had hundreds of items to test—a time-consuming and expensive process. They had to prioritize each piece of evidence according to how likely it was to be significant to the investigation. It was a slow task, but they were making their way through it all. The lab discovered nothing noteworthy on the vast majority of items. Police were disappointed to find that the slashed risers had many people's DNA on them, and it was impossible to pick out individuals from the mix. This was not completely unexpected. As well as Stephen's DNA, there would have been the DNA of anyone who had packed his reserve, as Stephen was not qualified to pack his own, as well as DNA from the first responders, and perhaps people who had been in the plane with him, given the close proximity in which skydivers are packed together. It was a blow that suspects could not be narrowed down this way.

One week later, police had no firm suspects and were no closer to making an arrest. They took the next step of sending a message to all 4,000 active skydivers in the UK. It said: "The investigation into the death of Stephen is ongoing. I am appealing for your help. Many of you will have known him and enjoyed his company socially and through his love of skydiving. Someone knows who committed this vile act and I ask that you contact me in total confidence. You may have opinions or information as to how Stephen met his death. Was he killed, if so, why? or would he ever contemplate taking his own life? I need to speak to as many of his friends and associates as possible. Please contact the incident room if you have any information that could assist us. I would also like to thank the many who already have. Sincerely, Humberside Police, Scunthorpe Major Incident Room."

The mention of suicide seemed to be just covering all

possibilities. Certainly, suicides were more common on the drop zone than murder—after all, what could be simpler or more finite than to exit an aircraft and not pull? Several people had taken that option over the decades, including skydivers who took the extraordinary path of actually climbing out of their parachute harnesses midair, one while his horrified friend filmed the event, unable to do anything to stop it.

Nothing in Stephen's demeanor in the ample video footage of that day suggested he was in any way suicidal. The jump itself was a spectacular success that would have taken a lot of concentration and coordination. What's more, Stephen deployed his parachute at the correct height and went through all his emergency procedures correctly. Suicides may be more common than murder, but it didn't seem like it was the case this time.

A FAREWELL FOR STEPHEN

Media scrutiny in the weeks following Stephen's death was intense. His parents made impassioned pleas for anyone who might know anything or may have seen something to come forward to police. They visited the airfield to see where their son's last days had been spent and to try and make some sense out of what happened. Police hoped the presence of grieving family members would stir the conscience of someone who was keeping a secret for a friend.

Stephen's teammates, Dave and Adrian, gave an interview to the press in which they relived the day their best-ever jump became a nightmare. They said Stephen had been bright and excited and in his normal buoyant mood before the jump. David felt guilty because he had been the one to do Stephen's gear check and had found nothing amiss. However, experts agreed that the tampering would not be revealed in a normal gear check. The damage to the main bridle would have only been evident by removing and inspecting the pilot chute, something no skydiver would have had any reason to do unless there was a reason to suspect something was wrong. Likewise, the damage to the reserve risers would only have been made evident by firmly pulling on them, an action that is not only not part of a check, but not recommended from a safety perspective, as it could disturb the pack job. Whoever had tampered with Stephen Hilder's parachute knew exactly how to hide the evidence from even experienced skydivers.

The media was soon reporting that the police had ruled out suicide because of Hilder's upbeat mood and his actions in trying to save his own life by setting his Cypres and going through emergency procedures. On July 12, 2003, *The Times* reported: "The police have failed to identify any suspects and skydivers are gripped by the fear that there is a murderer in their midst. A few facts are clear, say the police: the death of Stephen, 20, was neither an accident, nor suicide; this was not a prank gone wrong; and the killer is almost certainly a skydiver. He or she may strike again."

Skydiving returned more or less to normal, but the Hilder case was still a major topic of discussion around the campfire or bar after a day jumping. Because of the competition, there had been skydivers from all over the country at Hibaldstow that week, so the culprit could be a jumper at any one of the two dozen or so drop zones in the UK. Many skydivers began to change their habits, locking their parachutes in their car when they weren't using them. Hibaldstow Airfield installed lockers to take the place of the pegs in the common room for gear and some drop zones toyed with the idea of installing CCTV cameras in the hangars. Sales of tamper-proof gear bags soared, along with the paranoia of skydivers around the globe.

Three weeks later, the death of Stephen Hilder featured on the UK TV show *Crimewatch*. Police had not made any outward progress, but they believed that someone other than the person responsible knew something and were hoping that the show would encourage them to come forward. They also released video of the fancy-dress party, hoping it would jog people's memories or that skydivers would notice something that the police had not.

The TV show resulted in several telephone calls and a number of people had information about an argument at the party the night before. Most notably, two women provided a particular name, independently of each other. That name was quietly moved up the list of suspects.

STEPHEN HILDER WAS FINALLY LAID to rest on Thursday, July 31, 2003, four weeks after his death. The funeral service was held at St Mary's Church in Burghill, a village near Hereford. It was attended by hundreds of mourners, including skydivers, college friends, military personnel, and the investigating detectives. Adrian Blair joined the guard of honor and was one of the six pallbearers from the Royal Military College of Science at the Defence Academy who carried Stephen's coffin, draped in the Union Jack, into the church.

It was, as funerals often are, as much a celebration of Stephen Hilder's life as a mourning of his passing. The

Reverend Jimmy Morrison, who had known Stephen since he had converted to Catholicism at the age of seventeen, led the service, much of which concentrated on skydiving and his army career. Stephen's girlfriend, Ruth Woodhouse, recounted his love of amateur dramatics and his many humorous antics, drawing laughter from the crowd.

But there were some looking around the 300-strong congregation, wondering if there was a murderer among the mourners.

TWO MORE INCIDENTS

A month later, detectives were getting frustrated. They had been confident that they would uncover evidence in relation to the death of Stephen Hilder, but nothing had come to light. There were hours of footage taken by dozens of skydivers throughout the week. When a competition is running, there is always a camera filming something or other. Forensic tests were still being carried out, but nothing of note had turned up on any of the high priority objects that had been sent for analysis. They appealed for information from the jumping community about a competition Stephen had attended from May 2–4, around two months before his death, when it was believed he got into an argument with another skydiver. Detectives were sure that the answer lay in the skydiving community but were beginning to suspect that one or more people who knew something were not coming forward out of a sense of loyalty.

It was decided that fresh eyes were needed on a case

that was in danger of becoming stale. Humberside police appeared to have hit a brick wall, so on August 27, senior officers from across the UK were called in to review all the facts, evidence, and background in the hope they would spot something the locals had missed.

Detective Inspector Steve Clay, now in charge, said that police would write once again to all 4,500 registered UK skydivers, in the hope that the murderer had shared their secret. He was certain the killer was at the week-long parachute competition at Hilbaldstow where Stephen fell to his death in front of scores of witnesses. He said: "Our line of inquiry is that the murderer could have told a fellow skydiver about the dastardly deed."

Investigators had settled on a likely profile of the culprit, which they outlined in a police statement: "The person who committed this dreadful crime probably has no criminal history and is likely to be a well-educated young man with a bright future. There's little doubt that he will have shared the burden of what he has done with a loved one ... We are getting closer all the time. The answer lies among the skydiving community."

When the UK mailout didn't have the desired response, the next step was to take their inquiries worldwide. Police took out a full-page advertisement in *Skydive: The Magazine*, the leading magazine for the sport, asking for assistance in tracing the murderer.

In a chilling twist, US skydivers responded with the stories of two remarkably similar incidents of sabotage in 1996 and 1997, neither of which had been solved. Both cases technically remained open.

In the first instance, the parachute sabotaged belonged to champion skydiver, Kirk Verner. However,

Verner had loaned his parachute to a friend, Cary Hopwood, who had issues with his own gear. Hopwood had a double malfunction, but remarkably survived. Only one riser of the reserve parachute had been cut, which should have been enough to kill him, but the parachute managed to catch enough air to slow him down to a survivable speed. The unfortunate skydiver was left with permanent brain damage, as well as pins and metal down his entire right side.

The following year, in 1997, Charlie Mullins, the 25-year-old son of a well-known and controversial skydiving identity, discovered his reserve risers had been cut when he opened his reserve pack to swap it with a new one. If he had used it, there was no way he would have survived. Fortunately for Charlie, his main parachute had been left alone and he had no need to use his reserve.

In both cases, the men who owned the parachutes were the sons of drop zone and aircraft owners, which made them the envy of many. Skydiving is a notoriously expensive sport, but both Kirk and Charlie were able to amass thousands of jumps at a very young age thanks to their fathers, putting them at a distinct advantage when it came to competitions and professional jumping. Charlie had his first solo jump at the age of eleven, and by the time he was nineteen had an astonishing 5,000 jumps, more than anyone else his age. Although not close, the two intended victims moved in many of the same circles.

US law enforcement provided British authorities with the names of all those present at the time of the attempted murders in the US, as well as a video taken by Cary Hopwood of his own incident from the camera mounted on his helmet. It showed Cary trying to deploy and seeing his pilot chute float away due to the cut in the bridle, just as Stephen's would have. Cary then activated his emergency chute and it showed that one riser had been cut. The video showed Cary's hands reaching up and police heard his chilling shouts of "Oh my God, I'm gonna die," before he hit the ground.

Cary suffered numerous broken bones and a head injury that caused impaired vision. He had no recollection of the incident, nor could he recognize his parents or any familiar landmarks around his own home. He only partially recovered, and his life was ruined from the incident, with rumored drug and alcohol addictions and run-ins with the law later in life.

Both Kirk and Charlie returned to the skies, despite the fear that someone wanted to do them harm. Police had concentrated on one suspect, a disgruntled former employee of Kirk's father, but were unable to find enough evidence for an arrest. Now the US police hoped that a breakthrough in the Hilder case might lead to a similar advance in the US investigation which, after seven years, had gone cold.

Nothing came of it. The similarities in the cases seemed to be mere coincidence, and not a particularly surprising one at that. The method of tampering was one any experienced skydiver would recognize as being both completely effective and unlikely to be noticed. The fact that all three incidents used a similar modus operandi was most likely the simple efficiency of a murderous mind.

AN ARREST AT LAST

Another month went by. Another month of skydivers wondering if they were sharing an airplane with a murderer. Another month of heartache for Stephen Hilder's parents.

Police had not been idle, however. They had been following up leads and talking to people who had stories that may or may not have been significant. They had looked into an incident at another skydiving event a couple of months before his death, when Stephen was rumored to have had an argument with another jumper. Every piece of information had to be investigated, although most of them went nowhere. They expanded their interviews to hundreds of people, including family, friends, teachers, and fellow students from his time at Bristol University and the Royal Military College of Science at Shrivenham.

But then, on October 22, 2013—three and a half months after Stephen Hilder died—the police announced two arrests. The police did not release the names to the press, but Stephen's Commanding Officer contacted newspapers to let them know. The two men arrested were Adrian Blair and David Mason, Stephen Hilder's teammates.

Knowing the tight friendship between Mason and Blair, police had ensured they were kept apart and questioned separately. News of the arrests ripped through the skydiving community. Some condemned them immediately, stating they suspected them from the beginning. There were unsubstantiated rumors about a love triangle. Some spoke of David Mason having played pranks on Stephen previously, including one time when he tampered with Stephen's gear after he left it in the cloakroom. David had pulled out the pilot chute, causing the pin to dislodge and the main parachute to tumble out of its bag.

Skydivers had a mixed reaction to this incident. Some were angry that anyone would mess with another person's gear without their permission. On the other hand, it was not clandestine—Stephen could not have put his parachute on without replacing the pin and pilot chute first, so it was more annoying than dangerous. David said he had done it as a way of highlighting that Stephen had left his kit in an unsafe area, as a joking revenge for Stephen always being so strict with safety regulations.

After the initial anger, the skydivers adopted a wait and see attitude. One wrote on a popular skydiving forum, "These two are good friends and I have jumped with them many times. As someone who knows them, I am willing to give them the benefit of the doubt for the moment."

There was also the fact that the team had pulled off the jump of their lives that day. That would be an even more incredible feat if one or more people on the skydive had known that they were about to watch somebody die.

Mason and Blair were held overnight at separate police stations. The next day, police applied to the court for an extension to allow them to hold the two young men for an extra twenty-four hours. After forty-eight hours, they were released on bail without charge. The law in the UK allows suspects to be released on conditional police bail so that the police can pass their file to lawyers who act for the Crown Prosecution Service. It was up to the Crown Prosecution Service to review the evidence and decide if there was sufficient evidence to bring charges against them. This happens in cases when the evidence the police have is very marginal and they think they might be able to get a conviction but are not really sure.

Despite no charges being laid, Mason and Blair found themselves under a cloud of suspicion from the "Where there's smoke, there's fire" people. Their home drop zone, Netheravon, told them not to come back for a while. They were technically free, but until their names were cleared, going to any other drop zone would be uncomfortable at best and dangerous at worst. Angry skydivers might well take out their frustration on the kits of the two suspects. The two young cadets entered a period of limbo.

THREE WEEKS LATER, on November 17, police announced another arrest in the case of Stephen Hilder. A 24-year-old man from Leeds was taken into custody at Humberside police station and questioned on suspicion of murder and a separate offense of criminal damage. This time, no name was released to the press, nor did police say if the suspect was a skydiver. However, the arrest came two weeks after police interviewed members of Leeds University skydiving club, who regularly used Hibaldstow Airfield and were there during the college competition. The Leeds University student newspaper had the arrest as front-page news, calling the suspect "a man studying at Leeds."

After fifty-six hours of questioning, this man was also released on bail, but was to return to Scunthorpe police station at an undisclosed date the following year. His name was never released to the skydiving community.

Once again, all the police's inquiries seemed to be coming to a dead end.

A NEW THEORY

On December 5, 2003, one week before what would have been Stephen Hilder's birthday and five months since he fell 13,000 feet to his death, his parents made another impassioned plea, determined to keep his case in the media. There were a limited number of people who could possibly have carried out the sabotage on his parachute and police had DNA from them all. There had been three arrests and three people released without any charges being laid. Yet, detectives were still certain that the killer was known to Stephen and most likely struck in the heat of the moment.

One police officer told the press that Stephen Hilder had "one or two disagreements" with fellow skydivers in the week before his death. However, they said that several witnesses lied to them over the course of their investigation. One witness had falsely suggested Stephen had been involved in a love triangle, something that was not borne out by any facts.

Stephen's teammates, Adrian Blair and David Mason,

were officially released from bail, but Humberside police refused to eliminate them from the investigation. The third man remained a mystery, but police stated three dossiers on men who had been arrested were being prepared and would be forwarded to the Crown Prosecution Service in due course.

The Hilder family spent that Christmas, the first one without Stephen, still no wiser as to what happened to him.

By the end of January 2004, Humberside police had interviewed 2,500 people and still had no motive for Stephen Hilder's murder. Detectives set up in a room at the British Parachute Association's Annual General Meeting on January 24–25, hoping somebody would come forward with fresh information. The AGM was a two-day affair that included demonstrations of new equipment and talks from experts on different aspects of skydiving. As it was in the middle of winter, it was attended by a large percentage of the UK skydiving population, providing them with a skydiving fix while there were no drop zone operations. There was little new information for the authorities, but they took what they had to a conference near Scunthorpe on January 28 that was attended by the most experienced murder detectives in Britain, criminal and behavioral psychologists, along with experts in skydiving and forensics.

With no further information forthcoming from the skydivers that pointed to a potential motive or murderer, detectives turned back to a theory that had been briefly raised, then discarded, at the beginning of the investigation. Had Stephen Hilder committed suicide?

Police changed their line of questioning to family and

friends. Had Stephen given any indications that he could be contemplating suicide? Did he have any problems or challenges he was having trouble accepting? They knew his skydiving obsession had caused him to neglect some other parts of his life, including study and his girlfriend. Could that have affected him? How was he in the weeks, days and hours leading up to the jump?

They spoke with those who knew him best. His mother had spoken at length to him on the Friday before the competition and said he was his same, talkative self. He'd had a good time with his father at the Bon Jovi concert the Saturday before and with his girlfriend on the Monday. Nobody had noticed anything different in his demeanor. What's more, they were all adamant that Stephen would never take his own life. He was not the type to contemplate suicide.

THERE ARE no reports of what happened on the case over the next six weeks, but it was clear that the police had not yet finished with Stephen Hilder's teammates, Adrian Blair and David Mason. On March 10, 2004, detectives searched the rooms of both young men without warning. On David's computer, they found a draft obituary for Stephen, written in a humorous style, for a skydiving magazine. Although they did not reveal the contents of the obituary, police found it disturbing and inappropriate. David said the article was being misconstrued by police and was merely the black humor typical of skydivers.

The lawyer the young men had hired together told

the press that they were shattered. He said, "They were
taken aback when the police turned up out of the blue. I
don't know what the police were looking for. The boys
had no involvement in Stephen's death."

Whatever police were looking for, it seems they did
not find it. Two weeks later, to their great relief, Adrian
and David were notified that they were no longer
suspects and had been cleared of any involvement in
Stephen Hilder's death. However, the suspicion, uncertainty and relentless targeting took its toll on the young
men. Adrian quit his degree at the Royal Military College
and moved to the US.

WITH ALL SUSPECTS OFFICIALLY CLEARED and no others on
the horizon, police doubled down on the suicide theory.
Tests found DNA from the sweat on Stephen Hilder's
hands around the frayed edges of material that was
slashed on one of his parachutes. Assuming this referred
to the main bridle that had been cut, this discovery was
meaningless. It would have been far more surprising to
discover that Stephen's DNA was not on there, as sweat
would be expected to transfer onto the main bridle every
time the parachute was packed.

Further tests found minute fibers from the cut
webbing on the clothes that Stephen was wearing
beneath his jumpsuit. This was interesting, but inconclu-
sive, as he probably did his gear check before putting on
his jumpsuit, so any fibers that were on the outside of the
rig could have transferred then.

Then the proverbial smoking gun surfaced. A pair of

scissors that had been picked up from the locked trunk of Stephen Hilder's car and bagged was found to be the tool used to cut the risers. Not only did the scissors have fibers on their blades, only Stephen Hilder's DNA was found on them. The scissors had been given a low priority due to what was described as "a monumental misunderstanding" between police and British Parachute Association expert John Hitchin. When Hitchin was unable to cut through the risers with the scissors he was supplied, he asked for a hook knife. Police had understood to mean that scissors would be unable to cut through the tough material. However, the skydiving expert claimed he meant only that the particular scissors that had been given were unable to cut through, but other scissors would be fine. The scissors found in the trunk of Stephen's car were ordinary kitchen scissors in good working order.

Investigators also began probing further into Stephen's personal life. They heard about the time he told friends that if he was going to commit suicide, it would be by skydiving. There were reports that he was not enjoying his time at the Royal Military College of Science, as he was in a course he did not like and was under the impression that he had failed his examinations, although the college said that this belief was mistaken. Police found he had racked up £17,000 in debts and maxed out his credit cards, much of it on skydiving. He had bought himself an expensive, state-of-the art parachute. Skydiving kit costs a lot of money. Then there are the jumps themselves—you could spend £100 on a slow day, and it was easy to spend a lot more, especially when training for competition. Stephen's debts were bad enough that he had bounced a check in the mess hall, which got him into strife with his military superiors.

There was also Stephen's unexplained eleven-mile drive to a gas station on the Tuesday before his first skydive, despite there being gas stations that were closer to the drop zone. It was the kind of place you would have to deliberately seek out, and he apparently did not put any petrol in the car, as his tank was nearly empty when investigators looked at it later. This led to some speculation that he had gone to purchase drugs for the party, though there was no proof of any drug use.

Finally, despite giving his skydiving friends the impression that he was very much in love with his girlfriend, Ruth Woodhouse and their relationship was solid, their relationship was on the rocks, and they were at the point of splitting up.

As for why he would stage such an elaborate suicide, rather than simply not deploy his parachute, theories ranged from his conversion to Roman Catholicism, which regards suicide as a sin, to ensuring his parents could cash in any life insurance, or simply to ensure he could not back out of his plan.

Nearly ten months after that fateful day at Hibaldstow Airfield, Detective Superintendent Colin Andrews, head of the Humberside police investigation, announced that they were no longer treating the death as murder and would not be looking further for a third party in connection with the death of Stephen Hilder. He said that the three suspects who had been intensively interviewed had come through the questioning and he now accepted that none of them had any part of it.

Skydivers remained unconvinced. One skydiver

summed it up on the forum dropzone.com: "Come on people, we all know that no skydiver would ever commit suicide in this bizarre way ... This is total crap. The cops are stumped so they're covering their ass."

But as far as the police were concerned, the investigation was being scaled down to an "unexplained death."

DENIAL AND DISBELIEF

The police may have been satisfied with their findings, but nobody else was. None of Stephen's family, his friends, his girlfriend, or skydivers, whether they knew him or not, bought the story that Stephen Hilder had committed suicide and staged his own murder. It was not that suicides were unheard of—they certainly did occur, given the absolute certainty of death when jumping from 13,000 feet without a parachute. But to do it in such an elaborate manner, which would cast suspicion on innocent people, while showing absolutely no outward signs of nerves, depression, distraction, or concern was unthinkable.

Why, the skydivers asked, did he turn on his Cypres, the automatic opening device? Why did he go through all his emergency procedures, methodically, and at the right stages of the skydive? These were not the actions of a man changing his mind at the last second and frantically trying any method to save his own life, but the responsible, practiced actions of a seasoned skydiver who knew he would have to deal with a parachute malfunction one day. Most of all, no skydiver believed it would be possible to pull off the skydive of your life, under the pressure of competition, when you knew you had only had seconds to live.

As for the remark Stephen had made about dying by skydiving, that was a common comment within the community. It was more a reflection of how much people loved the sport, much the way someone might say, "If I'm going to die, I hope it's when I'm having sex." Nearly every skydiver had had that conversation at some point, and it was especially common for young and new jumpers to be adamant that it was the only way to go.

Several of his friends knew about his debts and said that he was not concerned by them. Like many 20-year-old men, especially those who had a guaranteed career ahead of them, he thought his debts would sort themselves out and he did not dwell on them. Many people of a similar age pointed out that they were not much more than average student debts that you would amass by attending college, if you did not have the military paying for you.

Ruth Woodhouse also said that the idea their relationship status could have caused him to be suicidal was absurd. Their relationship was a casual student affair, which grew from their mutual love of drama and doing a play together. Rehearsals meant they saw each other twice a week, but they could not spend enough time together for it to develop more deeply, especially as Stephen spent every weekend skydiving. Ruth said that neither of them were clingy people and there had been no distress or entreaties to stay together from either of them. Both were happy with what they had and the decision to split was mutual.

One friend posted on dropzone.com: "Steve was the kind of person who worried about something only when it was absolutely staring him in the face. His attitude was always 'it'll be OK', no matter how unrealistic that was. Splitting up with his girlfriend, being in debt and having possibly failed exams wouldn't worry him until the point where he'd been declared bankrupt, been chucked out of uni and seen his girlfriend with a new bloke!"

The scissors may have been found in the locked trunk, but the keys were in the ignition. All skydivers have gloves and many wear them when the weather is warm, because, even on the hottest day, it is very cold at 13,000 feet. They also guard against cuts and scrapes from bad landings. Seeing someone wearing gloves would not be at all out of place, even on a hot day. The fibers that were found on Stephen's clothes would have naturally been there just from handling his own parachute.

Finally, there was Stephen's demeanor in the weeks, days and hours leading up to his death. It is not unusual, according to experts, for someone who is suicidal to be upbeat after they have made the decision to kill themselves. But that would normally follow a period of depression, and there was nothing in Stephen's background or any time leading up to his death that had changed.

Stephen's closest friend, non-skydiver Jason Saunders, told the *Independent* newspaper that Stephen was full of plans for the future in the last conversation that they'd had just before he left for Hibaldstow. The newspaper reported: "The men discussed the amateur play they were due to perform in with the Royal Navy's amateur dramatics society and Mr. Hilder spoke excitedly about the possibility of joining the Navy after his training at the Royal Military College of Science in Shrivenham, Oxfordshire. The chat ended as it always did, with Mr. Hilder teasing his friend to overcome his vertigo and take his first skydive for a tandem jump he was organising to raise money for his college diving team, Black Rain, and as usual, his friend refused."

Stephen's mother had spoken to him on the Friday before he left, and she said he was absolutely normal and enthusiastic about the competition. His father, who had attended the Bon Jovi concert with him the next day, said "He was an energetic, enthusiastic, fun-loving and confident young man, planning for his future."

Few people bought the official police line, but they couldn't come up with a motive or any suspects, despite massive speculation on drop zones and online. The investigation had hit a brick wall.

INQUEST

I n March 2005, an inquest was finally held into the
death of Stephen Hilder. Press around the time
concentrated on the suicide angle, with headings
like: "Troubles drove skydiver to suicide, inquest told" or
"Skydiver's amazing death hint." The inquest was told
that the police investigations had led them to the "absolute conviction" that Stephen had not been murdered.

On the other hand, his former girlfriend Ruth was
adamant. "There is just no way. I've looked back on the
whole relationship and even in hindsight I couldn't find a
single thing to suggest he would have killed himself, or
why anyone would kill him." She also said that Stephen
was knowledgeable about forensics and, "If he was going
to stage something, he wouldn't just chuck the scissors in
the back of the boot [trunk]."

On March 23, 2005, nearly two years after the 20-year-
old fell to his death, the coroner returned an open verdict.
An open verdict is an official statement either saying that

a crime has been committed but not naming a criminal, or saying that there has been a death but not naming the cause of death.

Coroner Stewart Atkinson acknowledged that police had found no evidence that any third party had been involved in the sabotage of the skydiver's equipment. He added that he was unable to record a verdict of suicide because he could not be sure the skydiver intended to take his own life and forensics left doubt as to whether Stephen had tampered with his own equipment. It was thus an open finding.

Detective Superintendent Colin Andrews told the BBC he was as comfortable as he could be that Stephen wasn't murdered. He said he was "not complacent, but confident" and that the investigating team had left no stone unturned in the pursuit of the truth behind what happened.

The open verdict did not sit well with the skydiving community, few of whom believed it was suicide. Suicide or murder were the only logical possibilities, and although skydivers are realistic about death in the sport and accepted that the former would be much more common than the latter, the details of Stephen's case meant most believed it to be one of the very rare occurrences of homicide. The bigger question was whether Hilder was personally targeted or if it was a random act of sabotage.

Many in the UK skydiving community were left uneasy. One jumper said: 'The worst bit is if it was murder the person may still be among us. That freaks me out a bit considering the size of the active skydiving community ... There's only 19 drop zones in England, that means you've got a 1-in-19 chance of jumping at the same DZ as whoever did this, and no one yet knows who did this or why."

Nevertheless, as the news stories petered out, memories faded, and skydivers went back to their old ways. Visit any drop zone today and you will see unattended parachutes all the time. "Skydivers trust each other. We have to," Hibaldstow's chief instructor Paul Hollows told *Real Crime TV* when they ran a special in 2011.

But as in any community, that trust can be broken, and when it is, the results are devastating. In November 2006, a 26-year-old Belgian woman, Els Clottemans, was convicted of murdering her fellow skydiver and love rival by sabotaging her parachute in exactly the same manner as Stephen Hilder's had been. The two women had been in a sexual relationship with the same man, a fellow skydiver. Clottemans had sabotaged Els Van Doren's parachute after arriving at the man's house to find Van Doren in the bedroom. Van Doren recorded her own death on her helmet cam, the footage surviving the fall. Clottemans was jailed for thirty years.

In May 2015, at Netheravon, Stephen's home drop zone, army sergeant Emile Cilliers was arrested for attempted murder after sabotaging his wife's parachute. She suffered multiple serious injuries, including a broken spine, shattered pelvis, and broken ribs, but survived the ordeal. Cilliers was found guilty in May 2018 of trying to kill his wife to pocket the life insurance and start a new life with his secret lover.

However, mystery continues to surround the death of Stephen Hilder. His parents remain hopeful, that somebody, somewhere, knows what happened and may still come forward to give them closure.

In the meantime, all skydivers can do when they remember Stephen Hilder, who died two decades ago, is recite their well-worn refrain: *Blue Skies, Black Death.*

SECRETS OF THE THREE JACKS

WHERE'S RUSSELL MARTIN?

INTRODUCTION

2020

For forty-three years, Bev Roberts has written letters. She has written to police chiefs, to lawyers and magistrates, to coroners, and finally to the Missing Persons Action Network. In the curly cursive hand of a bygone era, Bev has begged them all for the same thing: "Please find out what happened to my brother, Russell Martin."

Most people just want her to let it go. The police have marked his file "inactive." Russell's former wife doesn't care what happened to him. His four kids barely remember him. The town where he went missing from—Stawell in country north-west Victoria, Australia—seems to think it was no great loss. "He was a hard man," say the old blokes who have been in the town for decades. Their memories follow a pattern: he was always getting into trouble; he treated his wife badly; he drank too much, gambled too much, fought too much.

Bev accepts that her brother was no angel. But she is getting on in years, and her health is beginning to fail her. Russell's brothers have passed away and, to Bev, it seems she is the only one left who cares that he's gone. All she wants before she joins her brothers is to get some closure on the mysterious events in a country town in 1977.

MISSING FROM THE GIFT

1977

The Stawell Gift is the biggest annual event in the region that sits about 150 miles north-west of Melbourne, the capital of Victoria, Australia. Every year since 1878, sprinters from all over Australia and further afield have descended on the country town to take part in the heats that culminate on Easter Monday in a 120-meter sprint across the grass of the local oval. It is the oldest and richest short-distance foot race in Australia and attracts thousands of runners, supporters, and punters for the weekend. It is a much-needed boost to the economy of the small town which, in every sense, is struggling.

In 1977, 37-year-old Beverley Roberts and her mother, Nellie Martin, awaited the Easter long weekend more anxiously than usual. The two women hoped that they would see Beverley's younger brother Russell, whom they hadn't seen since almost the beginning of the year. He had seemingly taken off abruptly one night, leaving his wife and four children to fend for themselves. That was not completely out of character for Russell. He was known to take off from time to time, and there was little anyone could do to stop him. But this time he had been out of communication for longer than usual, not contacting his mother, any of his siblings, his kids, or his friends. Russell had been born and raised in Stawell, and the town meant everything to him. It was where his roots were. Despite a tough upbringing and a hard-working, low-paying life, Russell loved the town, especially at Easter when the Stawell Gift was on. Bev knew that if her brother didn't turn up to place a bet on the Gift, something was very wrong.

The holiday weekend came and went. The Gift was won by Warren Edmonson—the first American to win the race since 1889. Russell Martin would have had plenty to say about that down at the pub afterwards. But Russell Martin never turned up.

RUSSELL MARTIN

R ussell Norman Martin was born in Stawell on July 10, 1945, to Michael and Nellie Martin. He was the sixth child in a family of seven, and his life was a struggle from the start. Both of Russell's parents were problem drinkers who lived a wild lifestyle, with little regard for their brood of children. They would stay out all night and not come home until their money had run out or they were escorted back by the police. Sometimes their drinking binges lasted for months. They fought loudly and often about their lack of money and Nellie's numerous affairs. Sometimes they would bring home all manner of people to the little house to drink, fight or fornicate, and it didn't matter if the kids were there.

Russell's older brother Michael later said of his parents: "They were never home; they sometimes stayed out for weeks. Us kids would have to look after ourselves. They lived a wild sort of lifestyle. They use to associate with people like Bill Moller who was my uncle and a lot of other drinkers in the town. They used to be referred to by some of the townsfolk as the Razor Gang."

Razor gangs were criminal gangs that dominated Sydney's crime scene in the 1920s. They were known for their wild ways and propensity for violence. However, Michael and Nellie's fights rarely got physical and they did not beat their children, although the kids knew it was best to keep out of their father's way until he sobered up.

Not surprisingly, child protection officers came calling often to the Martin household. The children became accustomed to recognizing them and ran into the nearby forest to avoid being taken away. Michael recalled: "Sometimes we would resort to sleeping in the bush night after night so they wouldn't be able to get us."

Sleeping in the bush and trying to take care of themselves meant they often arrived at school dirty and unkempt. Bev recalls Russell being teased mercilessly for coming to primary school with burrs stuck in his knotty hair. The only way he could get them out was to cut his hair, which resulted in a disastrous style that brought even more ridicule. Other children bullied him for being the kid of the town drunks, his lack of cleanliness and his academic struggles. Russell soon learned to retaliate to the bullying with his fists. He became known as a fierce fighter who wasn't afraid of anyone.

While Russell was still at primary school, his parents finally had enough of one another and called it quits on their marriage. That also meant the end of the Martins as a cohesive family. Russell's two older brothers, Trevor and Michael, stayed on the property with their father. Russell and his younger sister Wendy went with their mother to another address in Stawell. Bev and her two sisters moved to Kyabram to work in the cannery.

Nellie, Wendy, and Russell moved house often and Nellie had a lot of different relationships with men, some of whom moved in from time to time. One of the men was their uncle, Billy Moller, who was related to their father by marriage. Eventually Wendy moved out, aged 9, to live with her sisters. Then it was just Russell and his mother. Russell's wife would later claim that Russell told her that during this time he sometimes had to share the bed where his mother was sleeping with men. His uncle Billy was rumored to be his real father.

After drifting through primary school, Russell moved on to the local technical school. He left at around the age of fourteen and got the first of a string of tough manual laboring jobs, working at the Country Roads Board Quarry. As he grew into a young man, he continued to get himself into trouble and scrapes, and at eighteen had his first arrest and conviction for assault.

Trevor, Michael, and Bev Martin, having grown up in an alcoholic household and seen the damage it could do, all grew up to be non-drinkers. Russell, on the other hand, liked a beer as much as he liked a fight and did not follow in his siblings' footsteps. According to Michael: "Trevor and I didn't drink mainly because of what we had seen growing up, however Russell was different; he was a drinker and he developed a bit of a reputation for being a little bit wild. He learned to box and got involved in fights."

RUSSELL AND HELEN

I n the early 1960s, when Russell was in his late teens, he met Helen Wilcock, the niece of a former girlfriend of his older brother Trevor. Helen was a local girl who moved in some of the same social circles as Russell. She was considered a "wild child," and Russell's siblings who had remained in Stawell disapproved of the relationship. Trevor Martin claimed that Helen's parents had a hard time controlling her as she was very rebellious and got into trouble at school and at home: "I heard that her parents were concerned about the people who she associated with and some of her activities. I'd heard that she spent a lot of time at hotels around town."

When Russell sought his family's thoughts about asking Helen to marry him, all of them advised against it. Hot-headed Russell ignored their advice and on August 7, 1964, Russell Martin married Helen Dawn Wilcock. They were both nineteen years old.

Right from the beginning, it was a far from idyllic marriage. Russell and Helen, both products of disadvantaged backgrounds, drank, gambled, and fought constantly. Russell once presented with a deep head wound and Helen explained that she had accidentally hit him with an ax. Another time, he awoke to his bed in flames and accused Helen of setting him alight. Helen told him he had fallen asleep with a cigarette in his hand. They moved home often, and spent a few years away from Stawell, as far afield as Western Australia, as Russell chased available work. Helen recalls a couple of apartments in St Kilda, Melbourne, including a boarding house where the notorious Pentridge prison escapees Ronald Ryan and Peter Walker joined them to take refuge for a while.

However, whenever he was away, Russell missed his hometown of Stawell terribly and he returned as soon as he could. Russell and Helen lived in several different addresses, renting from family or friends. Helen had eight children in rapid succession, four of them dying soon after birth from a rare blood disorder.

The Martin men were all known to be hard workers, eking out a living with woodcutting and farming jobs. Although they lived in the same town, Russell was not very close to his more-conservative siblings. As Trevor stated: "Russell developed into a drinker and our interests became less common." Trevor and Michael both said they only saw Russell when he needed to borrow tools.

Russell and Helen's social life revolved around pubs and the local footy club. Russell played for Halls Gap, where he earned the nickname "Stabba." Most of Russell's mates came from the club. They played football on a Saturday afternoon, then followed that up with a social night in the clubrooms, at a pub, or someone's house.

Russell's wild ways continued. He was well-known to the local police, but not well-liked. They were called out to investigate complaints of noise and domestic violence at his house. He got pulled over for drink driving and was charged with refusing to provide his details after an accident. He was convicted of assaulting two police officers. Helen claimed there was one night that Russell got booked for driving while drunk, and he was so incensed that he grabbed a gun and went to wait for the cop who booked him to come home. Helen called another police officer, who, she claimed, just went and got Russell and brought him home.

One of the most enduring stories about Russell was the time he had gone to a bottle shop and was incensed by the slow service. Paul McDonald, Russell's young neighbor, was with him at the time. He told police: "We drove down to the Railway Hotel, which is now called the Gift Hotel. We pulled into the drive-in bottle shop and Russell waited in the car to be served. Back then the bottle shop wasn't manned all the time and no one had come out after five or so minutes. Russell got out of the car, went to the boot, and pulled out his shotgun. I remember him letting two shots off into the air in order to get their attention. The two shots got everyone's attention and a few people came out to see what was going on. Russell said something like 'If you're not going to serve me, I'll go around to the Brix.' With that, he got back into the car and drove around to the Brix."

It was common knowledge around town that Russell did not treat his wife well, and complained of her being no good at housekeeping or with money. It was not uncommon to see Helen with bruises or a black eye. But this was country Australia in the 1970s. Mateship was valued above all else, and nobody would dream of getting involved in a neighbor's business.

His children all claimed that he never beat them, though the youngest said he once caught his dad drinking the bottle of beer that had been left for Santa. According to Helen: "He never belted them or anything like that, never. Just... he didn't want to feed them either, and he didn't want to clothe 'em. My mother used to feed 'em and clothe 'em. But that was just his way. He had to spend his money on his gambling. But he was never too bad to 'em, no. He was never bad to 'em."

VALMA

In the early 1970s, Helen and Russell befriended a girl by the name of Valma, who was around eighteen years old and lived nearby. She visited often and sometimes watched the children while the couple were out.

Helen had had many complications with her pregnancies, and would be admitted to hospital for several months at a time. While she was in hospital to have Stephen, Valma moved into the house and began an affair with Russell, which Helen discovered when Russell failed to pick her up after the birth. From then on, Russell went back and forth between the two women.

Valma fell pregnant and gave birth to a little girl in September 1972. It was an open secret around town that Russell was the father. Over the next couple of years, Russell would periodically move out of the house he shared with Helen and their children to move in with Valma and her daughter. He would stay for a couple of weeks and then go back to his other family.

He seemed to enjoy playing the two women off against each other. At one stage he made plans with Valma to leave his family and run off with her and their daughter. Valma sold her car and collected her possessions from her mother's house in preparation for the move, but then Russell told her he had changed his mind.

Russell was very jealous and possessive about both Helen and Valma and couldn't deal with any other men paying them attention. Valma recalled one incident when they were out and she danced with another man. Russell later viciously assaulted the man in the parking lot outside the venue.

The two women knew about each other, but neither was in a position to complain. Helen would later tell police: "I can remember one day he brought Val Collins in, which she probably would have told you, and belted the livin' daylights out of me in front of her."

Helen would also say: "I felt sorry for the man, because he'd had a bastard of the life as a kid. I mean, he been belted and bashed, and bloody sleep with his mother in the bed, while his mother's with other... other blokes. And he's grown up with this hatred in his mind of all women, we're going to do the same thing."

At some point, Helen claimed she took out an intervention order against Russell. In a statement she said: "That was after he'd thrown me out of the house in Bennett Street in the middle of the night. And I went and got this house around in Ligar Street, not far from the one we lived in, couple of doors down, and he kept coming around there too, annoying me, at all hours of the night and morning, so I had an intervention order, and I went to court. I honestly don't know what kind, all I know it was an intervention order. That day he was delivered with the intervention order, he arrived at my place with Johnny Oates about 10 o'clock at night and I got a heck of a hiding that night for taking this intervention out. The police were called and they told me not to call them again, in future get in contact with the Commonwealth Police."

Whether Helen was lying, mistaken or the order was never filed, there is no evidence of any intervention order on record. Helen would later say she was often told by the police to shut up and stop calling them. She may have believed she was granted an order, when in fact she only asked for one.

Russell continued his relationship with Valma until 1975 when Valma met another man and moved away from the town. Also around 1975, Helen, Russell and their four surviving children moved onto a Miner's Rights block, which they acquired from the government, at 41 Ligar Street, a couple of streets back from Main Street in Stawell. There they lived in a little shed as they waited to have a three-bedroom house transported from nearby Ararat to put on the land. When the house was finally habitable, they moved in. The two girls had one bedroom, the two boys were in the other and Russell and Helen were in the third.

As he got older, Russell was treated for a possible psychological condition at the Pleasant Creek Special School, which was built for children, but accepted some adult outpatients. His symptoms included headaches and the regular feeling that he was choking. In February 1975, he was admitted as a voluntary inpatient at Lakeside Psychiatric Hospital in Ballarat for a few days. Russell was diagnosed as suffering from agoraphobia and treated with Valium and Serapax.

A NEW FOOTY CLUB

Later that year, some of the footballers including Russell, decided to break away from Halls Gap Football Club and re-form the Glenorchy Football Club, which had folded some years before. They recruited players and a new coach, Peter Ivey, a cop recently stationed at Stawell. Although Russell and the local police didn't tend to get along, he and Peter became good mates, arriving at training together, drinking afterwards and socializing with their respective wives.

Football matches were played every Saturday, either at their home ground of Glenorchy—a rural village with barely 250 people, about 10 miles north-west of Stawell—or at the grounds of their competitors. It was a struggling little club and they needed everyone to participate in some way. Helen volunteered to serve on the committee as secretary/treasurer. When the president of the club resigned, Russell stepped in to become temporary president.

Footy tends to be the heart of most small towns, but

players were scarce and they were lucky to get a full team on the ground. When the team was at risk of having to forfeit a game due to lack of players, they would march into the local pub and make every able-bodied man put on a jumper and run out onto the ground, even if they had never kicked a ball before.

The resurrection of the Glenorchy Club was not well thought out. The club struggled from the beginning, languishing at the bottom of the ladder. Russell, as was his way, clashed with other members of the footy club regularly. He came to blows with an electrician about who should pay for the wiring of the clubhouse. Around the club, as around town, Russell had the reputation of a man who should not be messed with, especially when he was drinking. He could turn violent over minor issues, and never backed down from a fight. It was clear by the time its second season was coming to an end that the club was not going to survive, and it folded once again.

It was not until the end of the year, when all the accounts had to be finalized and the coach and boundary umpires paid for their services, that club members realized that there was only a small amount of money in the bank account. It became obvious that someone had appropriated what little funds they had. Helen Martin immediately fell under suspicion as she was the club treasurer and person responsible for taking the money to be banked each week. Several meetings were called to get to the bottom of the matter, but each time Helen provided an excuse about why she could not attend.

Helen steadfastly denied any knowledge of the missing funds, although much later she would say that Russell used to help himself to any cash that was there for his gambling, with the promise that he would return it from his winnings or the following week's earnings. She always gave him cash when he asked because a refusal would turn into a fight and he would take the money anyway. According to Helen, Russell borrowed and repaid money often throughout the season, but in the end, he always borrowed more than he repaid. By the end of the season, there was almost no money in the bank account at all.

A TYPICAL BLOKE

Despite his fierce temper, gambling and alcohol abuse, Russell was not unpopular. He was typical of young men doing it tough in a country town built on hard labor. He enjoyed socializing and never missed an opportunity to bring out his piano accordion and squeeze out some tunes. He also took a keen interest in the business of beekeeping, something he inherited from his uncle (and rumored biological father), Billy Moller. Billy gave him several hives to get him started. Russell got his beekeeping license and made a small amount of money as an apiarist, though most of his meager income came from woodcutting.

People later said that of all the people in his life, Russell was closest to Billy Moller. The two men worked together, drank together, went duck and rabbit shooting together, and rarely a day went by that they didn't see each other. They used to argue over the fact that Russell only worked enough to subsidize his drinking and

gambling and would let his debts mount up. Billy sometimes got angry at Russell for not putting enough work
into his hives and threatened to take them back. Nevertheless, when times were tough, Billy paid off Russell's
debts. Over a period of years, he lent Russell over $12,000.
Tensions were always smoothed over and the two would
wind up at the pub sinking beers together.

Alcohol continued to be a demon for Russell. His kids
would later recall that, after particularly big sessions of
drinking, he would come home and tell Helen to put
them in their rooms. Then they would hear fighting.
Their oldest daughter, Lea, said that Helen sometimes
had black eyes or bruises after these fights.

One of the local police officers, Murray Emmerson,
stated that he "attended Ligar Street on numerous occasions. At times it would be a monthly occurrence."
Usually, his attendance would be as a result of being
called to a domestic situation, but charges were rarely
laid.

On October 24, 1976, Russell broke his ankle falling off
a Shetland pony in his own backyard. There were rumors
that he had broken it trying to get his dog out of the local
pound, but according to Helen, the illegal dog retrieval
happened shortly afterwards. She had driven him to the
pound, but when he jumped the fence, he realized he
couldn't get back over because of the plaster on his leg
and demanded that she find someone to help him out.
Helen went to her brother's house, where she found Peter
Ivey, Russell's footy coach and friend. Peter had been
helping Russell while he was on crutches by driving his
truck and assisting him with wood collection. Peter
offered to grab some bolt cutters and told Helen to go

home. Soon afterwards, the two men returned in Peter's divvy van [police divisional vehicle] with, according to Helen, not just Russell's dog, but several dogs from the pound in the back. He wanted to return them or set them free without a cent going to local council.

A CHRISTMAS HOLIDAY

On Christmas Day, 1976, Russell crossed the road to the home of Charlie and Dorie Stenhouse, who lived directly opposite. He needed to go to his in-laws for Christmas lunch but had no hot water at home. His neighbors allowed him to shower and shave, and he showed off the new clothes and watch that he had received from Helen and the kids for Christmas.

A few days later, Russell, Helen and the four children went on a New Year's camping trip to Lake Charlegrark, a couple of hours drive west of Stawell. Russell's sister Bev and her family joined them for the beginning of the holiday and Charlie and Dorie Stenhouse and kids arrived later. As usual, the focus of the holiday was camping and fishing.

Dorie Stenhouse would later recall that Russell and Helen had a huge fight a couple of days after she arrived. Russell stormed off down the beach and Helen followed him soon after, crying. They returned about half an hour later, but there was still tension between them. The next day, Dorie and Helen went into Goroke to have a beer. Helen was still upset, but she didn't tell Dorie what the argument was about. She told Dorie that she wanted to leave Russell, but she was afraid he would come after her and the kids with a gun. She also confided that Russell had been leaving the house late at night and she thought he might have found a new girlfriend to replace Valma, who had moved away.

The family returned to Stawell around January 13, 1977, and Bev went around to see her brother's new veggie garden shortly after. That was the last time she saw him.

During January, Russell continued with his woodcutting business, collecting, cutting, and delivering firewood. A neighbor, John Simmons, allowed Russell to collect and remove wood from his property for free. Russell worked hard cutting and preparing it for sale and left it at the property until it was time to deliver it.

On January 18, Russell attended his local doctor's office where Dr. Hayes reviewed his broken ankle. Everything seemed to be going OK and he made another appointment for a physiotherapy session on February 2.

That same week, Charlie Stenhouse visited Russell Martin at his home. He would later tell police that he found him in bed wearing only his underwear, with Helen placing icepacks on his head. Charlie described Russell as "delirious" and said he was only able to raise his head a small amount from his pillow. He looked at his neighbor and said, "Oh Charlie," before dropping his head back in exhaustion.

WHERE'S RUSSELL?

Charlie returned to visit Russell daily for the next three days. Each day, he was met at the door by Helen, who told him Russell was too sick to come out and that she didn't want to disturb him. Each time, Charlie thought that was fair enough and he went back home.

On the fourth day, Helen broke down into tears. She told her neighbor: "Oh I may as well tell you, Russell cleared off and left me on Monday. I've been telling you a lie about him being asleep. You'll hear about it from somebody else anyway, so I might as well tell you. He's cleared off and left me."

On Tuesday, January 25, Helen visited Bev to ask her to deliver some wood to one of Russell's customers. Bev thought it was strange that Russell had gone to the effort to cut a great deal of wood in John Simmons' yard, and had just left it there, when it was in a saleable condition and valuable. When Bev asked why Russell couldn't do it, Helen told her that he had taken off the previous Tuesday. He had been in bed all day, then at 11:10 p.m. he sang out asking the time and date. When she told him, he got up and said he had to go out for a minute. Helen went to bed and was awoken by Russell returning at 1:20 a.m. She said he picked up a pair of trousers, toothbrush, and toothpaste, put $100 and his watch on the bench and told her to sell that and anything else she needed. He said: "I can never come back to Stawell again. I'm sorry. I'm glad we had the holiday, it's the first in thirteen years." He told her to prepare for a couple of shocks. Then he went out the front door. Helen ran to the window and saw the back end of a white wagon or car. Russell got into the passenger side and the car took off.

It wasn't completely unheard of for Russell to take off for a while—days, weeks, but never months. The story sounded plausible enough, and Bev knew that he would be back. Despite his faults, he loved his children and couldn't be away from them for too long. Helen begged Bev not to tell anybody because chances were he had just been drunk and would be back and Helen would be humiliated if people knew that he had cleared off and left her again.

A few days later, Helen returned and told Bev that she had been mistaken about the day that Russell had cleared off—it had been on the Thursday, not the Tuesday as she had previously said.

Helen also began to cry as she told Bev that the footy club money had gone missing and that she believed that Russell had taken it. Bev wasn't close to her brother, but she certainly didn't want the family name dragged through the mud. She asked Helen how much had gone missing and then withdrew $1,000 from her personal bank account so that Helen could pay off the debts owed by the football club, insisting that she get receipts. Helen later gave Bev a receipt from an electrical retailer that had provided a TV for a raffle, and she said she had run into Peter Ivey who reminded her about the grocer's and baker's accounts. The total of the bills came to $924. Helen kept the remainder for incidentals, promising to pay it back at a later date.

A little while later, according to testimony provided by Bev, the two women bumped into each other at the local milk bar. They were discussing Russell and Bev's mother, who was in hospital, and Helen asked whether she had been told about Russell being missing. Bev said she had not, and Helen then said to her: "Well, don't tell her, I don't want her to get upset. Have you heard any talk?" When Bev shook her head, Helen allegedly said, "Isn't it good that nobody's talking?"

A few days after Russell had apparently cleared off, Helen pestered his brother Michael to clear up the yard with his plow as he had promised to do. Michael later told police that he did it for the sake of the little kids, not for Helen. He didn't like her and "didn't think she was a nice person."

When Michael arrived, he ran the blade over the yard, cleaned the grass up and leveled the ground. Although three of Russell's siblings lived in town, they were not particularly close and the news that Russell had taken off hadn't filtered through to his brother. Helen sat at the back doorstep smoking while he worked, and he was unnerved by the neighbors staring at him from next door. He expected Russell to come home while he was there, but his brother never showed. When he finished,

Helen paid him $10, without a word about her missing husband, and he went home none the wiser.

Over the next week, Helen busied herself with cleaning up and returning tools and other items Russell had borrowed from his family. When they asked whether Russell would need the tools when he returned, Helen responded that he wouldn't be back. This came as a surprise to his brothers, as Russell was Stawell born and bred, and they were certain he wouldn't be able to stay away for long. That night, his brother Trevor went home to his wife and joked that he didn't think they'd be seeing Russell again because Helen had killed him.

A week or so after Russell went missing, Helen applied for maintenance and welfare for her children, Lea (11), Kelly (7), Steven (6) and Paul (4).

Over the next few weeks, Helen began selling off Russell's things. She sought out buyers for his farm machinery and vehicles. Billy Moller, Russell's uncle, rumored biological father and best friend, claimed that he gave Helen $500 not to sell off Russell's machinery because he would need it when he returned. He encouraged his nephew Kenny to buy Russell's bee boxes because Billy didn't want them to go to "just anyone."

Kenny thought it was strange that Helen was selling off things so soon after Russell had gone missing. It was almost like she didn't expect him to come back. Kenny agreed to buy the boxes to keep his uncle happy. When he was loading the boxes, Kenny noticed some had blood on them. He asked Helen about it, and she said it came from a pig they had slaughtered a few weeks earlier. He put the bloody box with the others, and piled them all into a shed, not sure what he was going to do with them.

On March 15, Helen purchased a 1969 Mazda 1500 Deluxe for $1,900, getting just $350 as a trade-in for Russell's Valiant Pacer Coupe. The dealer remarked that the 6-year-old Valiant was in very bad condition, despite having been cleaned thoroughly by Helen. It had both interior and exterior damage and was mechanically average. Helen was happy to offload it for the upgrade.

A NEW MAN

Around the end of March, Helen met a man called Mick Miller at the Railway Hotel. Mick worked on the railways and had relocated to Stawell a few weeks earlier. They hit it off well and left the pub together. Helen drove Mick home to his hut on the railway track, which was the accommodation provided by the railway. Four beds in each hut provided little privacy, so Mick followed Helen to her house in Ligar Street in his green Mini Minor. He waited in the car while she put the kids to bed and they slept together that night, Mick staying until he had to go to work. Mick returned to Helen's house the next night, and the two began a relationship. Within two weeks of meeting Helen at the pub, Mick moved into the house in Ligar Street.

Russell's sister Bev was shocked about the new relationship and confronted Helen, asking whether she had heard from Russell. Helen told her she had tried to report him missing at Stawell Police Station and the police officer Graham Brandt had told her: "He's over 21, he can

look after himself." She was told that Russell was probably with another woman, but she assured Bev she would
call her cousin, Sergeant Royce Weir, who was in
Melbourne's Accident Appreciation Squad, to see if he
could locate Russell.

From then on, the two women had nothing to do with
each other. Bev was sure that Russell would be back for
the Stawell Gift, and she was curious about what he
would make of all the changes that had come about in a
mere few months. But the Stawell Gift came and went
with no sign of her brother.

On May 3, 1977, Bev accompanied her mother to
Stawell Police Station where they made a missing persons
report. For Ellen Martin, the Gift was solid proof that her
son had not merely taken off. She had grave fears for his
safety and believed that if he were still alive, he would
have contacted her or his children. She admitted that he
had a violent temper and had a lot of domestic trouble
with his wife, and believed that, if her son returned to
find that Helen had moved another man into the marital
home, he would do serious bodily injury to them both.
She told police Helen was aware of this and the only way
she would have a new boyfriend would be if she knew for
sure Russell was never coming back.

Bev felt that Helen had been behaving suspiciously
ever since the holiday at the lake. She said that Helen had
left the campsite a few times over the ten days they were
there, without good explanations. She believed Russell
was still on crutches at the time of his disappearance,
which would make leaving under his own steam difficult.

Senior Constable Richard Kennedy, who took the
report, was familiar with the Martins, who had been

involved in several disputes over the years with local traders. Invariably, Russell had been summonsed over a debt owed for his business and he would claim that he had given the money to Helen, who was supposed to pay the bill. Helen would agree that Russell had given her the money and she had not passed it on. Kennedy said later in a report: "I have always found her to be a cunning type of person, and a poor manager of money." He didn't seem to leave room for the idea that Helen may have said what her husband wanted her to out of fear.

The detective got right onto it. At 3 p.m. that day, he and Sergeant Weir-Smith went to the Bull and Mouth Hotel where Helen worked and interviewed her for almost two hours. Helen repeated a similar story to the one she told Bev, but added that Russell appeared to be upset and may have even been crying when he said: "I've just got to go... Sell everything; the swing saw, the chain-saw, everything." When Helen asked him where he was going, he said he couldn't tell her, but repeated several times that she should sell everything to see if she could get herself out of debt.

She said she couldn't remember what he was wearing, but he had grabbed a pair of jeans, one pair of good trousers, a couple of shirts, and asked her to get his underpants and socks. He put all the clothes in a paper grocery bag from the local supermarket. He took no toiletries, nor did he take his new wristwatch, which was a Christmas gift from Helen.

She said Russell had seemed to be in a great hurry and left the house just a few minutes after he had gotten home. He had driven himself home and parked in the back yard, but left through the front door. Helen went to the bedroom window when she heard a car door slam and saw the back of a white panel van, or similar vehicle, with one, or maybe two other people in it. That was the last Helen Martin ever saw of her husband.

A fortnight later, she saw a similar white panel van parked out the front of her house, with a man in it. She first noticed him at 7:30 p.m. and he stayed there all night. Helen was too frightened to go out and see who it was, but she took down the numberplate details. She said she took three sleeping tablets at around 2 a.m. because she was so worried about the man in the car. She claimed to have called the police, but they accused her of lying.

Helen said she had heard several rumors about Russell since he had gone. Someone told her that he had been staying in Mount Isa, and others said that he was at the Mount Tom Price mine in Western Australia, thousands of miles away on the other side of the country. She'd heard that his mate Alan Frame had taken him to either Perth or Sydney. She also heard that he had been selling drugs and someone else told her he had run off with Valma Collins again. Another person suggested he was in a mental hospital at Ballarat. Nevertheless, she admitted she had not made any attempts to find him.

Even though it was Russell's mother and sister who reported Russell missing and Kennedy who took the missing persons report, when it was tendered in court sometime later, Bev noted that there were two documents filed. One was signed by Kennedy and the other by Peter Ivey. Both claimed that Helen had made the report.

Senior Constable Kennedy did not feel that Helen had been completely frank with him and set about making inquiries of Russell's family, friends, and neighbors. Helen's cousin Royce Weir denied her claim that she had ever come to him to let her know of Russell's disappearance.

When he heard Michael Martin's story about cleaning up Helen's yard a few days after Russell had gone missing, Kennedy wondered if she might have been trying to get something removed or was creating a diversion for later anticipated inquiries.

Charlie Stenhouse relayed the story about visiting Russell the day after he went to the doctor about his ankle, when Russell could barely raise his head. Charlie was certain he could not have left home that night under his own steam. Officer Kennedy felt that Charlie was sincere in his recollections. It seemed that, other than Helen, Charlie was the last person to have seen Russell.

Dorie Stenhouse claimed she heard a gunshot "about 3 days before Russell was supposed to have disappeared." Dorie had a clear memory because it frightened the hell out of her. She thought it was louts with rifles on the street. She spoke about it the next morning with another neighbor, Mavis Johnson, whom Dorie claimed said she had also heard it. When police spoke to Mavis, she could not recall a gunshot and told police that she did not want to be involved.

Dorie also repeated her tale about Helen and Russell's fight at the lake but couldn't remember if he was still on crutches at the time. She also remembered Helen leaving the lake a few times, to go into the local town of Goroke to get food, and she also returned to Stawell twice to collect mail and pick up a mattress.

The investigation found evidence that Helen had gone from door to door asking friends and family for

sleeping tablets around the time that Russell went missing. At least two people stated that they had provided her
with tablets and there was some implication that she had
never done this before. Because it was some months later,
nobody could remember the exact date this had
happened. Helen would later say that she did this in the
week after Russell went missing, because she couldn't
sleep.

Several people mentioned the missing cash from the
Glenorchy Football Club, with most of the suspicion for
the loss being on Helen.

Officer Kennedy spoke to Alan Frame to follow up
Helen's claim that she heard he could have taken Russell
interstate. Alan and Russell played footy together and
drank in many of the same pubs. Alan said that he had
been to Sydney around that time, but he didn't take
Russell with him.

Another rumor doing the rounds was that Alan had a
hastily installed concrete slab laid at his house shortly
after Russell went missing. The story went that he
engaged two local blokes to do the job cheaply. After
putting up the frame of the building, Alan realized he
had got what he paid for. The slab had too many cracks in
it to build on and the building was abandoned. He had
never sought a permit, so the council had not been out to
inspect the slab and frame. Rumors abounded that
Russell could be buried beneath that slab. Senior
Constable Kennedy noted in his report: "I feel that Frame
knows more about the disappearance of Russell Martin
than he would like the police to know."

There was one thing that everyone agreed upon. In
his report, Kennedy wrote: "I have established one thing.

And that is that all the persons I've spoken to, including both his friends and his family alike, all have one definite opinion. This is that if Helen had any idea that Russell was coming back, she would not have had another man in the house because Russell would kill them both."

A MOTIVE FOR MURDER?

T here was no doubt Helen had more than one of the usual motives for murder. She was trapped in a marriage where her husband beat her, with four children, no money and nowhere else to go. He had made it clear he would harm her if she tried to leave. He carried on affairs with other women. He drank and gambled away money meant for bills. However, Helen was not a large woman, and there was no way she would have been able to dispose of a body on her own. She would have needed help. None of her children were old enough or big enough to have assisted, so if she had been involved, so was someone else. But who?

RUMORS BEGAN to swirl around the town as the locals realized that there was a police investigation into Russell Martin's disappearance. Some people assumed he had just cleared off, some believed that Helen had killed him, and others thought that the local police had something to do with it. Like many country towns in the era, there was significant friction between the men who were doing it tough and law enforcement, and Russell clashed with them more than most. But there was no specific incident that anyone could recall that would have been a catalyst for such drastic action.

The location of Stawell on the edge of the Victorian goldfields, meant that there were hundreds of deep disused mine shafts that could conceivably conceal a body. One deep pyrite and gold mine, known as There Jacks, was just a mile out of town. Locals would often illegally dump rubbish and other junk down the mine shafts. One local claimed that the police used the closest mines as a dumping ground for old numberplates, rather than attend to the paperwork, and the local kids made a game of fishing them out with magnets and string.

One name that was brought up frequently was Peter Ivey. Peter and Russell were good mates who played footy together, and Peter had helped Russell out by driving his truck for him when he broke his ankle. However, they had been known to fight, with a particularly bad one not long before he disappeared. Some people believed that Peter and Helen were having an affair. When police asked Helen about it, she was adamant in her denial, saying: "God, no. No way. No. He had a lovely wife. No way known."

When queried, Peter Ivey denied ever having been in a fight with Russell, despite several witnesses claiming to have been there when it happened. Helen also confirmed that Russell had told her about the incident.

Police returned to interview Helen after speaking to

the people who knew Russell. One detective noted that Helen "appeared at ease and was obviously not worried about where her husband may be." She denied that Mick Miller was living with her, but admitted he was her boyfriend and that she wasn't sure what Russell would do if he came home and found them together. She conceded that he might try to injure her or Mick. Records showed that Mick had not arrived in town until February 27, a few weeks after Russell had disappeared, so he was unlikely to have been involved in any foul play.

Helen was evasive about the missing money at the footy club, though she said that she had been left with many debts, which she was paying off in installments. The detective concluded: "Further enquiries revealed that amounts of money had obviously been appropriated from club funds probably by Mrs. Martin."

When detectives interviewed Helen's brother, Phillip Wilcock, he was unable to assist with the likely whereabouts of Russell, but he did have something to say about his sister's credibility. He said that his sister was a compulsive liar and he kept clear of that part of the family as much as possible. It was apparent to detectives that he didn't trust Helen and thought there was something strange about the whole affair.

A couple of people brought up Russell's psychiatric history and his treatment for a nervous complaint at the special school, suggesting it could be the reason for him going missing, or perhaps harming himself. Dr. Hayes described Russell as suffering from "mental hysteria." Police were able to confirm that he had been treated as a psychiatric patient, but his records were confidential.

Local gossips were sure that certain people were

having affairs with certain other people. Secondhand information morphed into firsthand stories. Everyone had a theory or knew someone who knew something but finding genuine information among the conjecture was a difficult task.

With no apparent leads or physical evidence that a crime had been committed, the investigation petered out.

Helen and Mick's relationship continued, with neither of them apparently worried about Russell returning home and finding them together. Helen sold the saw bench and the tractor and most other things around the house that had belonged to Russell. She used some of the proceeds to pay off the debt collectors who continued to call.

INVESTIGATIONS GOING NOWHERE

In May 1978, a year after making the first missing persons report and Russell having missed another Stawell Gift, Russell's sister Bev hired a solicitor in a last-ditch effort to get some answers about her missing brother. Bev's finances were limited, and she could not afford much more than a basic search, which was carried out by Highland Investigators. They interviewed Helen and found some minor discrepancies and deviations from her earlier stories, but there was not enough to reinvigorate the investigation.

From time to time over the years, tales circulated that Russell had been spotted somewhere. A man named Wayne Yole told Russell's mother, Nellie, that he had seen Russell at a cafe in Swan Hill, and that he was fine and not to worry. Later he admitted that it was a story he had concocted with the publican where he was staying because Nellie Martin was coming in so often and lamenting about her missing son. They made up the story to take the pressure off her.

Russell's uncle, Billy Moller would go around to hotels and show Russell's photo to locals to see if any of them had seen him. When he heard rumors that Russell was camped by the Murray River, Billy went to check. When Russell was sighted in a nearby town, Billy went to check. Billy kept searching until his death a couple of years later. His nephew Kenny told investigators: "Any little thread he could grab to, he always looked into it to see if there was any evidence anywhere. He'd grab it and look into it and he couldn't find any basis of any truth of why he went there."

In 1979, Russell's mother Nellie passed away. Russell loved his mother and was fiercely protective of her despite his painful childhood. Those in town who believed Russell had merely nicked off thought he would return for her funeral. Those who believed him to be dead thought that this occasion would prove their theory beyond reasonable doubt. If Russell was alive, there was no way he would miss his mother's funeral.

When he didn't turn up, even the most open-minded concluded that Russell Martin had probably met an untimely end. It was enough of a reason for the police to give the investigation one last look. On June 6, 1979, Sergeant Holcombe, who took over Russell's missing person file a year earlier, interviewed Helen. He put a series of allegations to her, along with discrepancies and inconsistencies that had emerged during investigation.

It was a long and probing interview, but at the end Sergeant Holcombe said: "I was not able to draw a conclusion as to the true circumstances of the disappearance of Russell Martin. There was no evidence at that point of time on which a prosecution based on a standard of proof of beyond reasonable doubt could be commenced."

Investigators conducted searches with government agencies, banks, and utilities, but none could provide any records for Russell Martin. With no body and no hard evidence, Russell Martin's case went cold. His file was marked inactive, and most people assumed that he was dead.

LIFE GOES ON

Helen and Mick's relationship lasted several years before they split after an incident of infidelity on Mick's side. Soon after, Helen started a relationship with Charlie Smith. Charlie was a local slaughterman with a checkered past. In 1967 he spent a month in prison for an assault on the son of a police officer in the backyard of a pub. In 1974, he was charged with the abduction with intent to carnally know a girl between ten and sixteen years. On February 1, 1974, he was acquitted of the abduction but convicted of carnal knowledge. He received a two-year sentence but was released after nine months. While still on parole, he got a job carting logs with local logging contractor Freddy Cooper and he and his wife moved to Stawell.

Charlie claims to have met Helen when she was a barmaid at the Bull and Mouth. He was still married to his former wife when he started a relationship with Helen, but the marriage was already on the rocks. It is unclear whether they knew each other previously, as they lived nearby and had many mutual friends. In particular, Charlie was good friends with Alan Frame, and the pony that Russell fell off belonged to another of his close friends, Peter Perry.

Charlie moved in with Helen and her four children at 41 Ligar Street. The couple married on September 10, 1983, and Helen took on the surname Smith.

Little by little, Russell "Stabba" Martin faded from the town's memory.

IN 2001, twenty-four years after Russell went missing, further inquiries were made ahead of an upcoming coroner's inquest into the circumstances around Russell's disappearance. Detectives reinterviewed people who had a connection with the case or a story to tell.

A couple of people told a story they claimed to have heard either directly from, or about, local panel beater, Bill Joyner. Bill often repaired damaged police vehicles. The story went that a police officer had come to Bill in the middle of the night and insisted that a repair be done urgently and privately. The repair was a large dent in the bonnet of the car. The dent might have been made by a kangaroo, but that didn't account for the secrecy of the job. One man swore that it was a "human shaped" dent. Unfortunately, by the time this story circulated, Bill Joyner was deceased and could not be called upon to confirm or deny.

Then there was the party. As time went on, people in the area swore there was a wild party the night that Russell went missing. At this party, they said, Russell had a massive fight with Peter Ivey. They also said he went out and came back with a knife, which he threw in the sink, and declared that a local man by the name of Danny Marks "wouldn't be using that again." But it seemed that these were misremembered events. The party was apparently to mark the end of the football season, which would have been months before Russell went missing. Danny Marks claimed not to recall any such incident at all. And Charlie Stenhouse, who by this time was deceased, had previously sworn that there was no way Russell could have gotten out of bed the day he went missing under his own steam, let alone be well enough to attend a party.

Detectives interviewed Kenny Moller, the nephew of Billy Moller, who had bought Russel's bee boxes from Helen after he went missing and had noted blood on one of the boxes, which Helen told him was pig's blood. On January 30, 2001, police attended Kenny Moller's house to get the bloodstained bee boxes from his shed where they had been sitting, almost forgotten, ever since he had bought them. Homicide detective Mark McCann recalled in a later statement: "I opened the front door up and noted that there was furniture and other items stacked from the floor up to and beyond the height of the rafters entry beyond one metre was not possible without removing items of furniture. There was a large amount of dust and cobwebs that covered the entry. I formed the opinion that no one had entered the shed for some years, a stack of planks of wood cover the rear double doors, which had obviously been there for many years. We removed the timber and opened the rear doors of the shed to find it stacked with bee boxes, frames, and honey tins.

"Once again, due to the amount of dust and cobwebs, it was obvious that these doors had not been open for some years. Several of the bee boxes had the number M 437 engraved into them, which was Russell Martin's beekeeping license number. Other boxes, had the name Russell Martin on them, written in texta. We emptied the majority of the contents of the shed. However, we were unable to find the specific boxes with the blood on them that Kenny Moller had referred to. We did find two boxes and some frames with a red substance on them, but Moller did not believe them to be the boxes, to which he was referring to in his statement. On the first day of February 2001, I took the boxes and frames with the red substance on them to the VFSC, where they were examined. Biologists were able to confirm that it was not blood on the boxes and frames."

On March 8, 2001, Detective Mark McCann interviewed Russell's wife, who now went by her married name, Helen Smith. He later mentioned some inconsistencies in Helen's statements, saying: "She said to Mrs. Roberts that there was $100 left on the bench whereas to Mr. Whiteford she denied this. There's some talking about being in debt, yet on 15 March 1977 she purchased a new vehicle. There's an allegation that two males turned up from Ararat and wanted to purchase some drugs from Russell. Now throughout the entire investigation, there has never been even a hint or a suggestion that Russell was in any way involved in drug use other than prescription drugs. She allegedly told people she had reported him missing when that clearly was not the case. Finally, she said on the day that he went missing that he was sick and vomiting in the gutter, yet that day he actually went to Dr. Hayes for his ankle and Dr. Hayes never makes any mention of him having any other illness, which I believe is inconsistent."

On 14 March, police interviewed Alan Frame about the hastily laid slab on his property for a structure he never finished. He denied any knowledge of Russell's disappearance, but police officers felt he was hiding something.

On March 21, police attended with scientists from Monash University to carry out a geoscope search on the slab at Alan Frame's house. It came up with a negative result, so there was no justification to dig up the slab.

CORONER'S INQUEST

I n May 2002, the case of Russell Martin's disappearance was brought before the Coroner's Court to make a finding about the most likely thing to have happened to him. By this time, the four Martin children were grown up and had varying levels of interest in finding out what happened to their father.

Lea, the oldest, was in Grade 6 when her dad went missing. She had not been home at the time, but away at school camp. When she got home, Helen had told her that Russell was on holiday. Lea said she continually asked her mother where he was and when he was coming back, but Helen never spoke about it. Lea had concluded later in life that he was still alive, and when asked how she thought her mother felt about him leaving, she said: "She was probably relieved because dad used to hit her."

Kellie, the next oldest, didn't remember Russell, and all she knew of him was that her mother said he was "an asshole." She was keen to find out what happened to him, but was quite sure he was dead. She believed the rumors around town that the local coppers had something to do with it.

Stephen was about seven when his father went missing. He said that he never heard his mother talk about his father. He believed she knew what happened to his father, but he told the coroner: "She might know something but I know there's a lot more people who know a hell of a lot more."

Paul was not yet four when Russell went missing and couldn't remember anything about his father. Sitting in pubs, he heard a lot of the old blokes say the coppers had "given him a hiding" and thrown him down a mine shaft.

Family, acquaintances, and police gathered at the Coroner's Court to provide or listen to evidence about what happened to Russell Martin all those years ago.

There were many differing memories of the same incidents from the various witnesses, but some were just rumors rather than their own recollections of what had happened twenty-five years earlier. Some people seemed to want to inject themselves into the drama, while others wanted to minimize the role they had to play.

Kenny Moller was grilled about statements he had made to put suspicion on Helen, such as the suspected blood on the bee boxes and a secondhand report that a truckload of dirt had been delivered to her house shortly after Russell disappeared. Both stories were false, or at least exaggerated. In fact, Michael Martin testified that he had *removed* a truckload of dirt from Russell and Helen's house.

Some people testified to having witnessed acts of domestic violence by Russell to his wife, but they hadn't felt it was their place to intervene.

Helen's ex, Mick Miller, testified that there had never been any discussion about Russell in the house when he moved in with Helen and her children shortly after Russell went missing. The kids never mentioned him, and Helen had never indicated that she was concerned about Russell returning home. He did hear a bit of gossip around town that Russell was a violent and possessive man, but he didn't take much notice of it. This was much to the disbelief of a lawyer who said: "Are you asking this court to believe, Mr. Miller, that you take up with a married woman shortly after the disappearance or leaving of her husband and you don't ensure that you have some sense of security in being there?"

To which Mick Miller responded: "I can only answer your question. If you don't want to believe me, it's not my problem." When the lawyer continued to put scenarios to him and question how he could be so relaxed about the matter, Mick finally responded: "At the time I was slinging a ten-pound sledgehammer for probably nine hours a day and I was reasonably fit myself, so it just didn't particularly bother me."

Russell's son, Stephen Martin, said that the court should hear from local police officer Murray Emmerson, who was known to have had bad blood with Russell. According to Stephen: "Well there was just a time when he went to get his divvy wagon fixed at Bill Joyner's and it was the early hours of one morning and he had blood and everything over the front of the divvy wagon, with a dint in the front of it." He was reminded that his mother, Helen, had said that the panel van that she had seen Russell get into had not been a police divisional wagon. When asked what he thought the connection was between the divvy wagon and his father's disappearance he responded: "Well I don't know. It's for youse to find out."

Russell's brother Michael was suspicious that Helen was having an affair with both Peter Ivey and Billy Moller. Of the latter he said: "He give Russell the bees and give him everything, give him the world, and he was always there and he was a single man and I seen what was going on with my own parents, by the same man."

At the inquest it came out that Detective Holcombe had kept tape recordings of his interview with the neighbor, Charlie Stenhouse, and a covertly taped discussion with Helen Martin. He told the court he retained the tapes for safekeeping for over twenty years, a somewhat unusual move for a detective. When asked why he said: "If at any stage consequent to the conclusion to my investigation Russell Martin was found or his body or remains were found, there would then possibly be further continuing investigations into the matter. As I had conducted substantial investigations I considered that I'd be one of the first that the police would consult with concerning my investigations and I wanted to ensure that if that situation arose that copies of all the documentation and the tapes were available for further investigations."

Peter Ivey seemed to have a terrible memory. He couldn't recall any fights or arguments with Russell, he couldn't remember any parties, he couldn't remember the incident at the pound, he couldn't remember when he became aware that Russell had disappeared. He couldn't recall whether he spoke to Helen about Russell's disappearance, he couldn't recall whether Russell ever had an affair and he didn't know whether there was any domestic violence in their marriage, although when pushed, he said: "Well, from my recollection they did have a fiery type of marriage, they were a fiery couple."

Peter couldn't remember whether he thought there was anything odd about Helen selling off Russell's things within days of him leaving and moving another man into the house within weeks. He couldn't remember if he ever booked Helen for speeding. He could not explain why his name was on a missing persons report that he didn't take and why Helen was named as the person making it, which she never did. He couldn't recall whether anyone at the station asked for his assistance in the missing person case, given that he knew the family better than anyone else there.

He was, however, emphatic in his denial that he had ever had a sexual relationship with Helen: "No, I didn't and—there was no—you know, I think if you ask anyone from the club or anyone anywhere no one—that amazes me that anyone's ever said that, because I can't think of any situation that I've ever been in where someone would think something like that."

In his testimony, Sergeant Kennedy cleared up the matter of Helen being named on the missing persons report. He said that after they received the report from Russell's mother, they were instructed to talk to his wife, and after they did so, they put her name on the report. He couldn't explain why there were two reports, one of which had been signed by Peter Ivey.

Russell's youngest son, Paul Martin, testified that he had recently been approached by an Aboriginal man who claimed to know where Russell Martin's body was. He said the man had taken him to the location the night before, but that he had been unable to find it on his own that morning. He claimed only to know the man's first name, which he would not reveal because he did not want to get the man in trouble with police. He said that he hoped the man would take him during the day, and then Paul would show the police the location.

The next day a homicide detective told the court that members of the State Emergency Service attended an area at Green Lake where they located two sunken areas in the ground. They commenced digging for approximately one foot and there was no indication that anything or anybody was buried there. Apparently, the unnamed man had come across the site fifteen years earlier and thought that it could be a burial site of somebody, given that the ground was sunken in two areas.

Detective McCann was questioned extensively, having taken over as lead detective on the case. He told the court: "I believe that Russell Martin has been murdered. And I further believe that Helen Smith has more knowledge of it than she has led the court to believe thus far."

Helen's new husband, Charles Smith, was called to the stand. He testified that Helen had once told him that her former husband left one night and hadn't been seen since. He said that sitting in court was the first time he had heard that anyone thought Helen had something to do with it. He said he'd heard all kinds of rumors over the years, but never had any interest in delving further into any of them.

During cross examination, Charles was grilled about when he first met Helen, as he and Helen had always maintained it was several years after Russell went missing. Alan Frame had claimed that Charlie and Russell had known each other from the pub, but as far as he knew they had no problem with each other. Charles said that he could not ever recall having met Russell. He was shown a photograph of his son in the newspaper from February 4, 1977, at an event that may have included the Martin daughters. When questioned about his statement, he said that Helen's eldest child was around twelve when he moved in. Lea would have been twelve in 1978—years before the two claimed to have met.

When Helen was put on the stand, her responses were equally vague. Asked whether she was concerned about Russell returning when she had moved on with another man, she said: "I was always concerned about him returning, yes. But I had to live my own life too." She denied having any involvement in, or knowledge of, any foul play against Russell.

ON JULY 5, 2002, Coroner Timothy John McDonald handed down his report. The coroner made the finding that Russell Norman Martin's death occurred on or about the 20th of January 1977 at an unknown place of unknown unnatural causes.

He further found that he had no reason to disbelieve the testimony of the now-deceased neighbors, the Stenhouses, about seeing Russell shortly before he went missing in a delirious state in bed.

The coroner went on to say that he found the evidence given by Russell's former wife Helen, her current husband Charlie, and former police officer Peter Ivey to be unconvincing and evasive. He said: "I am satisfied that the witness Peter Claude Ivey was not a frank, open or truthful witness in the evidence that he gave to the court. I did not accept that a person who was a police officer and who played sport with Russell Martin, and drove his truck to assist him when he had a broken ankle on the 24th of October 1976 would have such little memory of the details surrounding Martin going missing on her about [sic] the 20th of January 1977. He was an unreliable witness.

"Further, I am satisfied that Charles Eugene Smith knows more of the circumstances surrounding the disappearance of Martin than what he has told investigators and this court. He was an evasive and vague witness who was hard to pin down to give clear and definitive and definite evidence. He was equally vague in a record of interview conducted with him at Stawell on 8 March, 2001. Smith has indicated to investigators that he had little or no knowledge of Russell Martin at the time of his disappearance. He says he may have met him at a hotel at some time, but cannot recall this. This is inconsistent with the evidence of Alan Frame, a good friend of Smith... Because of the unreliability of Smith's evidence. I'm unable to accept his assertion that he was not known to Helen Martin prior to the 20th of January, 1977.

"Helen Smith has also been vague, unclear, and misleading in what she has told different people about the circumstances of her husband's disappearance. Examples of this include saying that she had reported to Thomas Weir, then a member of Victoria Police that her husband was missing; telling Beverley Roberts different accounts as to when he left the house, and the different stories she told Charlie Stenhouse. Further, the evidence before the court is that during her marriage to Russell Martin, he engaged in a relationship with another woman who had a child to him. During this relationship, Russell Martin would return to the matrimonial home at times and continue his relationship with his wife. This was allowed to occur because of the fear that these two women had for Martin. This fear was well founded, as it is common ground that Russell Martin was violent toward his wife. She's attested to this fear in evidence. What I'm satisfied of is that the behavior of Helen Martin, very shortly after she says her husband left home, is consistent with her knowing that he would never return. Other than Martin saying that her husband told her he would not be returning, there is no evidence before this inquest for the court to find that it would be reasonable for Helen Martin to believe that this would be the case. Reasons for reaching this conclusion are the evidence before the court is that Russell Martin loved his children. He had strong family, and other ties in Stawell. Whenever he had left the matrimonial home on other occasions, he had always returned. Witnesses have given evidence that he would not leave Stawell, without ever having some contact with the people he loved. There is no reasonable explanation before the court as to why he would want to leave Stawell permanently.

"I am satisfied that Helen Smith has not disclosed the true circumstances surrounding the disappearance of her husband to the court. Further, I'm satisfied that she possesses information that is likely to establish such circumstances. After taking into account all of the evidence before the court. I'm satisfied that the disappearance of Russell Martin on or about the 20th of

January 1977 was associated with suspicious circumstances, and that he died on or about that date from causes that were not natural."

Russell's sister Bev was pleased with the coroner's findings, but she was disappointed to discover that it didn't mean her brother's case was going to be reinvestigated or that any consequences or arrests would flow from the inquest. An inquest is not a trial. The coroner does not make findings of guilt or apportion blame. All they can do is try, as best as possible on the evidence put in front of them, to discern the identity of the person who died, the time, date, and location where the death occurred, make a summary of the evidence relating to the circumstances of the death, and in some cases comment or make recommendations aimed at preventing similar deaths.

Although the coroner's report concluded that Russell had died "of unnatural causes" and that one or more people knew more than they were saying about the circumstances around his death, there was no new information that warranted his case being reopened.

HOPING FOR ANSWERS

Bev Roberts continued to write letters and make phone calls, undeterred by the many walls she came up against. Still hoping for some closure in her brother's death, Bev provided a DNA sample to be crosschecked with unidentified human remains at the Victorian Institute of Forensic Medicine. There were no matches. She tried every avenue available to her to have her brother's case heard or investigated and she meticulously noted, filed, and reported every piece of new information that came her way.

A person can apply to the coroner to have a case reopened if there is substantial new information available. Bev tried several times over the years to have Russell's case reopened, most recently when a local man came forward with a claim that he had seen Russell put into a divvy van by a known local policeman, never to be seen again. The claim, however, did not match up with timing information known to be true, such as Russell's last doctor's appointment. In March 2020, Bev received a letter from the Coroner's Court saying they couldn't take the matter any further.

In response to whether police would continue to investigate, the coroner's letter said: "Detective Senior Constable Anna Dickinson recently advised the court that police had made further inquiries as a result of information provided to them in 2018 ... DSC Dickinson advised that these inquiries have now been exhausted and therefore the police investigation is currently considered inactive."

In June 2021, Bev Roberts passed away, having never discovered what happened to her brother. Her son said one of his mother's greatest regrets when she passed away was still not being able to lay her brother to rest. "I promised her I would never stop looking for him, for her," he told the *Stawell Times*. "I intend to keep that promise. I want to honour my mother and keep searching for answers which might lead to finding him. No family should have to go through not knowing - I saw just how much it tormented my mother over the years."

The old blokes who gather at the pubs around Stawell, the ones who have claimed the same seat at the bar for decades, still remember Stabba Martin. His disappearance provided years of gossip, rumor, and speculation. They nearly all have an opinion, vague though it may be, that his wife and the coppers killed him and disposed of him down the Three Jacks, a mine that is less than a five-minute drive from the house on Ligar Street, long since filled in with several truckloads of concrete. If Russell is there, he's staying there. It would take a very expensive mining operation to recover a body.

Helen and Charlie live in the same forest as the Three

Jacks mine, on a dirt road, isolated from their neighbors. Helen still insists she has no idea what happened to her former husband: "I don't even like thinking about all these memories. I've got a good husband now who's really good to me and I'm very happy...I think he just took off. He'll be somewhere—I don't know about now, but he was all right when he left."

DEAD END DRIVE

THE MYSTERY OF DANNIELLA VIAN

A LOST PHONE

At approximately 7:30 a.m. on the morning of Wednesday, July 18, 2018, Julie Dykes Thomas received a call from an unfamiliar number. The man on the other end of the line introduced himself and told her that he had found a phone and, having seen baby pictures on it, assumed the owner would want it back. Still not quite awake and confused about why the man was calling her, Julie soon established that the phone in question belonged to her 25-year-old daughter-in-law, Danniella, whom she knew had planned to go out partying the night before. Julie thanked the man and asked him if he could drop the phone off at Danniella's workplace, the Asian-themed chain restaurant PF Chang's in the Bel Air Mall in Mobile, Alabama.

Julie was not alarmed by the call. This was certainly not the first time Danniella had lost a phone and probably wouldn't be the last. Still, Danniella would be happy that it had been found and so, as soon as the onsite office of Danniella's apartment complex opened at 9 a.m., Julie called the building manager and asked them to leave a note on Danniella's door to say that Julie knew where her phone was. Danniella would see the note when she woke up, or came home, whichever the case might be.

Later that day, the man called Julie again. He said: "Hey your son Tyler just called, and I explained what was going on, and he wanted me to get back in touch with you." Julie knew Tyler must have been trying to call Danniella from prison, where he was serving time for drug-related crimes. He called Danniella often from jail and would have been suspicious to hear a man answer her phone.

Julie responded to the man, saying: "No I still haven't heard from her, thank you for letting me know. I've got your number, I'll let you know if I hear from her."

When the man heard Julie's response, he asked her to meet somewhere, but Julie had neither the time nor the inclination to meet a strange man to pick up her daughter-in-law's phone and again asked that he drop it off at the restaurant, where they would keep it until Danniella arrived for her shift.

There was still no cause for alarm. Danniella had bought a new car just the day before, which provided her with some much-craved freedom, and Julie knew that she had gone out that night to celebrate the purchase. It would not be unusual for her to stay at a friend's house after a night out, and the loss of the phone was completely in character, especially if Danniella had been on a bar crawl.

At around 4 p.m., Julie went to Danniella's apartment. The note she had asked the building supervisor to pin to the front door was still there. Danniella was not home, and it appeared she had not been home since the previous day. Julie guessed the celebrations must have gone on until late and Danniella was sleeping off a hangover at a friend's house.

With her habit of losing phones, Danniella had come to learn Julie's mobile number by heart, so Julie assumed she'd call in at some point. If not, she would turn up at Julie's house the next day when Cora—Danniella's daughter and Julie's granddaughter—was due to return from a visit to her relatives. The 4-year-old had been gone for more than a week. If there was one thing Julie knew for sure, it was that there was no way Danniella would miss her little girl's homecoming.

The next morning, Thursday, July 19, the man who had Danniella's phone called again. Julie was becoming irritated and a little confused that this man, who apparently had simply found a random phone, kept calling her and had not dropped the phone off where Danniella could retrieve it. As he seemed reluctant to take it to the restaurant, Julie told him: "You just hang onto it, and when Danniella gets in touch I'll let you know and we can figure it out from there. We'll see what Danniella wants to do."

The man asked her: "Should we be worried?"

Julie assured him that it was completely in Danniella's character to lose her phone and stay out at a friend's place, and that there was nothing to worry about. Danniella would be fine. When she finally got off the phone, it struck her as very odd for someone who was apparently a stranger to be so concerned.

Later that day, Julie welcomed home her husband, Patrick, and their 4-year-old granddaughter, Cora, from their week-long visit to Patrick's family. Cora had been living with Julie and Patrick almost since she had been born. Despite their best efforts, Danniella and Tyler were unable to provide their daughter with a stable home life. The pair had an off-and-on relationship that was sometimes punctuated by violence, and Tyler's stints in prison had become a frequent occurrence. Most of the young couple's problems stemmed from Tyler's drug issues. Even though he was her son, it was Julie and Danniella who were as close as mother and daughter, especially as Danniella was estranged from her own mother. Julie called Danniella her daughter-in-law, even though Danniella and Tyler had never married.

Cora was full of chatter about her trip, which Julie listened to over lunch. As the afternoon wore on, Julie kept expecting Danniella to come through the door any moment. She couldn't help feeling annoyed that Danniella had chosen today to be running late. She often turned up late without calling to let people know, eventually arriving with some reason for her tardiness. However, Julie had expected Danniella to be on time today. Cora was eagerly awaiting her mother's arrival so she could tell her about the holiday.

By the time Thursday night rolled around, Julie was officially worried. Danniella had completely missed Cora's homecoming, and the little girl was now tucked safely away in bed without so much as a goodnight kiss from her mother. Despite the other issues going on in her life, Danniella was always loving and reliable when it came to her daughter.

Knowing that Danniella didn't have her phone, Julie tried messaging her on Facebook, which was Danniella's preferred method of contact. Julie kept checking to see whether her daughter-in-law had responded, but the little blue tick never changed into Danniella's avatar to indicate the message had been viewed, and the "last active" notification was now stating it was two days since she had logged on. When Danniella didn't show up that night, Julie became downright concerned. She decided the very next morning she would make a missing persons report.

DANNIELLA VIAN

D anniella Vian was born on March 8, 1993, in Roswell, New Mexico, to her mother Joy and a biological father she never knew. When she was very young, her stepfather, Bill Vian, adopted her and she took his surname.

Growing up, Danniella had a reasonable rapport with her stepfather. Bill was in the military, so the family moved around often. On the other hand, Danniella's relationship with her mother, Joy Vian, was tumultuous. She told friends that, when she was young, she felt less like a daughter and more like an accessory for her mother to show off. According to Danniella, as she moved into her teens, her mother came to view her as a competitor and demanded she stop wearing make-up and skimpy outfits. Due to their clashes, Danniella spent much of her teenage years couch surfing and staying with friends while the Vian family was stationed at the military base at Fort Riley in North Central Kansas. Later, Danniella would adopt the Instagram username @formerstreetkid, a reference to her teenage years, although whether she was kicked out of home or was transient by choice is not clear.

Fort Riley, on the Kansas River, is one of the largest and oldest military installations in the US, and home to many military families. It was here that Danniella met Tyler Sean Thomas. The two teens were part of the same circle of friends, an ever-changing group as kids came and went, something that was symptomatic of a military upbringing.

A military life means following the enlisted parent from base to base, which are sometimes hundreds or thousands of miles apart. These disruptions can mean a constant loss of friendship ties, and people without a knack for making new friends can become very lonely. Children who suit the lifestyle grow up to exhibit very resilient personalities and exceptional social skills. Others, however, struggle to develop and maintain deep or lasting relationships with other people or connections to specific places.

Danniella was pretty, independent, and bubbly, and was able to make friends with relative ease. Tyler Thomas was born on Christmas Day, 1990, making him a couple of years older than Danniella. They had a lot in common. As military brats, they had both developed the necessary resilience and ability to adapt, at least on the surface. They had grown up in the Bible Belt in families that believed in God, guns, and patriotism. Both had absent fathers, and stepfathers who had taken up the slack. Tyler had been adopted by Patrick Thomas when he was a baby. He never knew his biological father, who was out of the picture by the time Tyler was six months old.

A defining aspect of the "military brat" is that their lives revolve around the enlisted parent. One of the strongest bonds among the group is the common feelings of pride and admiration instilled in them for that parent, as well as the fear of losing them if they are deployed into active service. As stepchildren, teens like Tyler and Danniella might not have felt that particular bond as strongly as other military kids did, which gave them another reason to be drawn to each other.

Although the military brat subculture brought them together, there was no immediate romantic connection between Tyler and Danniella. In fact, Tyler married another girl within the group when he was around eighteen years old. That marriage went the way such very young marriages often do, and was over almost before it started. Soon after, Tyler followed his stepfather's footsteps and signed up for the military himself.

Tyler's military career saw him stationed in both Iraq and Afghanistan in a communications role. He kept in touch with his old circle of friends via social media, and in particular with Danniella Vian. As well as having a shared history and being part of the military life, the two found they had other things in common, such as an interest in tattoos and having better-than-average artistic talent.

When Tyler returned to the US, he barely greeted his parents before making a three-hour trip to visit his old friend Danniella Vian. Her family, too, had finished with military life and had settled down. Their rekindled friendship quickly turned to something more, and they officially started dating when Danniella was around eighteen and Tyler barely in his twenties, and quite likely still married, although no longer in touch with his wife. Tyler would spend another six months in the military before he was discharged.

As soon as he was finished with the army, Tyler asked Danniella to move with him to Mobile, Alabama, where his parents had settled. The city is one of haves and have-nots, part of the Bible Belt, with a deeply conservative culture. The overall crime rate in Mobile is 126 per cent higher than the national average in the US, with violent crimes such as rape, homicide, and aggravated assault trending upwards over the past ten years. Mobile has close to the highest crime rate of anywhere in Alabama and almost double the national average murder rate. In Mobile, you have a 1 in 17 chance of becoming a victim of any crime, and a 1 in 132 chance of becoming a victim of a violent crime. It is the sort of place where the Ku Klux Klan actively campaigned for Donald Trump, letter-boxing residents about the dangers posed by immigrants. The city has a history of economic swings, with much of its income coming from a robust domestic and international shipping industry through the Mobile Ports. Mobile residents can find relief from the hot and humid weather in nearby Mobile Bay or the Mobile River Delta, or travel half an hour to the Gulf of Mexico and the beautiful beaches of Gulf Shores and Dauphin Island. The most popular activities in the area, besides hunting, all tend to congregate around the water—sailing, fishing, kayaking, swimming, diving, or just hanging out on the beach.

When Tyler asked her to come to Mobile with him, Danniella didn't hesitate. She didn't feel any strong family attachments and seemed eager to distance herself from her mother and stepfather. Still very young and with no money to speak of, they moved in with Tyler's parents, Julie and Patrick, and his brother TJ.

From that moment, Danniella had only sporadic contact with her own family, preferring to blend in with the Thomas family and becoming especially close to Tyler's mother, Julie. For her part, Julie felt like she finally had a daughter after living in a household of men.

Right from the beginning, the relationship was anything but smooth. Tyler had not been the same since he got out of the military. He suffered depression and PTSD and did not respond well to conventional treatment. Instead, he turned to self-medication; specifically, he turned to a cocktail of drugs, culminating in a heroin habit. Tyler was no stranger to police and had been arrested for various felony and misdemeanor offenses. Danniella would sometimes turn up to work with bruises and other signs of domestic violence, causing her colleagues some concern.

Danniella and Tyler's relationship had all the hallmarks of a young couple who were both trying to deal with demons in their past. Although Danniella had no interest in heroin, she was not completely unfamiliar with drugs. She enjoyed a joint and would use amphetamines to keep herself alert, especially when she was pulling double shifts at work.

Despite the many rough patches, Danniella and Tyler loved each other and were also each other's best friend. They both liked tattoos, which they designed themselves, and over time Danniella acquired several, including a mandala-style flower on her left shoulder, a gray outline of an elephant on her right wrist, an outline of a heart, a

Buddha, and an American flag with a unicorn where the stars should be on her inner right thigh. On her left collarbone were two graveyard headstones sitting side-by-side, nestled companionably together. Inside the tombstones were the words: "To die by your side."

A BABY

With such a tumultuous, on-and-off relationship and chaotic lives, Danniella and Tyler did what many young couples in the same situation do. They had a baby.

They discovered they were expecting in early 2013. Determined to make a go of their relationship and provide a good life for their newborn, they got their own place in Mobile and prepared to become a family. The western neighborhoods of Mobile were characterized by pawn shops, payday loans, dollar stores, Fast Food chains, and billboards advertising "no win, no fee" personal injury lawyers. Danniella and Tyler went dumpster-diving together to furnish their apartment.

The young couple were genuinely close. They were good friends as well as lovers and both wanted to be good parents. Their daughter Cora was born in late 2013, but Danniella was found to have marijuana in her system while giving birth, and for her first month of her life,

Cora was placed in the custody of her new grandparents, Tyler's parents Julie and Patrick.

For a while Danniella and Tyler made it work, but it soon became evident that their own house was not a healthy environment for their baby girl. Although Danniella yearned to be a good mother, the only way she felt she could be one was to let Cora stay at Julie and Patrick's house most of the time. Tyler's heroin addiction continued to be the main cause of stress on their relationship. He got arrested several times and went in and out of rehab. The two of them fought constantly, each accusing the other of infidelity, and the shouting sometimes turned into physical altercations.

Danniella bounced around a number of different jobs in restaurants and bars around Mobile, including a stint working at Hurricane Grill and Wings, better-known as simply "Hurricane's." Hurricane's was a typical chain offering pub grub and alcohol, with a vaguely tropical theme.

Danniella made friends easily enough, being an outgoing and independent former military brat, but with her busy work schedule, her friends tended to mostly be workmates. In order to keep going through double shifts, she sometimes turned to Vyvance, a prescription amphetamine used to treat ADHD, similar to the better-known Adderal. As well as increasing alertness and decreasing appetite, Vyvance can cause the user to become jittery and anxious. It is tightly controlled, as it can easily be abused and cause dependence. Danniella didn't have a prescription, instead sourcing it illegally, through local drug dealers.

On March 25, 2015, during one of the many rough

patches in their relationship, Tyler filed a petition for custody of Cora against Danniella. In it he wrote: "I have been the sole provider for Cora since she was born. I am the only parent with a driver's license and the only parent with a steady work history. I have gathered evidence of her using drugs around Cora and evidence of her being unfit as a mother. I have been doing everything in my power to have contact with my daughter and it has been denied. I do not plan on keeping Cora from her mother. I simply need a way back into my daughter's life."

When the case came up in family court in October and Tyler failed to appear, the judge dismissed the application and awarded costs against Tyler. Cora was living with Julie and Patrick, and they started to discuss taking on full custody of her. Danniella missed having Cora with her all the time, but she knew the stability that Tyler's parents could provide was in the best interests of the child.

2015 and 2016 were rough times for the young couple, and their relationship was more off than on. Tyler's heroin addiction worsened, and in early 2016 he went to prison for breaking and entering. This was his first long stint inside, despite numerous previous arrests, all of which he had managed to bond out with Julie's help.

When Tyler was in prison, Danniella's friends urged her to forget him, reminding her there were plenty of other fish in the sea. Danniella had a couple of brief relationships and even moved in with one of her new boyfriends, after Tyler went back to prison for dealing heroin.

Despite the toxic nature of their relationship, Danniella kept being drawn to Tyler, giving him chance after chance. She told her concerned friends that Tyler was not just her boyfriend and father to her daughter but had been her best friend for seven years. Tyler was spending a lot of time in prison, but even when they were not romantically involved, when he was free, they lived in the same apartment. They remained friends throughout all Tyler's issues, even if they couldn't make it work as a couple. One of Danniella's friends called her Tyler's enabler when it came to his drug use.

ANOTHER BABY

As 2017 came to a close, Tyler was in prison, continually failing the drug tests that were a condition of his probation. When he moved to rehab, he was allowed out one day a week, and he and Danniella would spend that day together. When he was released again, Danniella told him she was pregnant. Tyler was overjoyed and vowed to stay clean so they could finally create a functioning family, until the couple attended the doctor and it became clear that Tyler was not the father. Nevertheless, he told Danniella he loved her and would support her throughout the pregnancy, until she gave the child up for adoption. The couple kept the pregnancy a secret from Tyler's parents, who now had Cora full time and had applied for full custody with, they say, Danniella's blessing.

By December 2017, when Danniella's pregnancy had started to show, Tyler regressed and lashed out in anger and humiliation at being faced with proof of Danniella's infidelity. The situation became untenable for Danniella and she decided to try and reconnect with her mother, Joy, who was living in North Carolina. Danniella wanted to go back to college, and work toward some sort of future for herself and Cora and perhaps the new baby as well. She wanted to get away from her life, away from Mobile, and put some distance between herself and Tyler. Cora stayed behind with Julie and Patrick. The move was short-lived. Danniella and her mother fought, and, missing Cora and absence making her heart grow fonder for Tyler, Danniella moved back to Mobile.

Upon returning, Danniella started work at PF Chang's, a casual dining restaurant chain with the sort of Chinese food made for Western tastes that would never be found anywhere in China. PF Chang's is one of those places that is affordable for most people and has pretentions of being upmarket, but in reality is overpriced for the quality of its food.

One of Danniella's fellow servers, Hannah Jakoboski, took the new girl under her wing. When Danniella told her she didn't have a car, Tyler having written it off sometime earlier, Hannah offered her a ride home, and the two were delighted to discover they lived just minutes from each other. They struck up a friendship and Hannah gave Danniella a lift to and from PF Chang's nearly every shift, even if Hannah wasn't working herself. The two women were similar in many ways and when Hannah started attending cosmetology school, Danniella was only too happy to help out. Although she hadn't finished the course herself, Danniella was knowledgeable, especially when it came to hair, and she was happy to let Hannah try out crazy colors and styles on her. She enjoyed changing her own hair color often, and at various times had been blonde, brunette, raven, red-haired, blue-haired, green-haired, and sometimes multi-colored. When she wanted more practice, she dyed her white cat, Toulouse, blue, using a natural, organic dye so as not to harm him.

Danniella worked almost every single day and often pulled double shifts to save up enough money for her maternity leave, but also in the hope she would one day be able to afford a car. A car would give her freedom and the ability to see Cora whenever she wanted and the chance to take her daughter out on excursions.

Danniella's pregnancy was becoming impossible to hide. The baby's father had no interest in raising the child but had offered financial support if she wanted to bring the child up herself. Instead, Danniella had decided she would give the child up for adoption. With the blessing of the baby's father, Danniella opted for an open adoption, where she would be able to meet potential adoptive parents for her unborn child. She was given details about numerous couples in the area who wanted to adopt. Danniella found a couple she was happy with, a police officer in Mobile and his wife, who was a teacher.

On June 6, 2018, Danniella Vian gave birth to a baby boy. The adoptive parents joined her during the birth, and she let them cut the cord, hoping that would help form immediate bonds for the new family. Although she was giving him up, Danniella wanted what was best for the baby. The adoptive parents were open to the child knowing who Danniella was, but Danniella didn't think it would be a good idea, as she wasn't going to be a part of his life. Alabama law provides that the birth mother can change her mind up to five days after the adoption, but

Danniella told Julie that they had an agreement that she would have the option to change her mind up to six months later.

As well as the adoptive parents, there was another person supporting Danniella during the birth, although he almost didn't make it. Despite wanting to be there for her, apparently Tyler couldn't face the situation without a hit. He overdosed and passed out in his car, but by fortunate coincidence Julie drove by and found him. She got someone to call an ambulance, which arrived equipped with Narcan. Narcan is a drug that negates the effects of opiates immediately, pulling the user out of their stupor and canceling out any high they had. It is so effective that many addicts abuse paramedics who use it on them, claiming it is a waste of their heroin.

The Narcan did its job and Tyler was immediately functioning normally and on his way to hospital as though nothing had happened. He was there to support Danniella through the birth of her little boy, before turning himself in to be put back in prison for once again violating his parole.

The evening of the birth, at 6:05 p.m., Danniella messaged Julie to say she was sore but OK. She wrote, "I'm good, just healing up. I've been resting this entire time. I had him at 2am. 7 pnds 11 ounces, everything is perfect with him. I haven't seen him. I've been thinking about it but I haven't made up my mind yet."

Danniella wrote a letter for her son, which she gave to his adoptive parents to give to her son upon turning eighteen. Then she left the hospital without holding her baby boy.

A GIRL'S GOALS

Despite her assurances to Julie about her health, Danniella had experienced some physical difficulties during labor and there were complications that continued after she left the hospital. She was in a great deal of pain and was bleeding heavily for longer than she should have been. Nevertheless, three days after the birth, Danniella was back at work. She was on a mission to save money toward her goals, and she may also have wanted something to distract her from the fact she had just given up her baby son. She pushed herself hard and didn't give herself time to heal. Instead, she relied on Norco, a strong painkiller she had been prescribed, which is used to treat moderate to severe pain. It is similar to the better-known Vicodin and can make the person who takes it drowsy. Users are warned to never mix it with alcohol.

It seemed the birth of her son and Tyler being back in prison spurred Danniella to take stock of her life and work toward a better life for herself and her daughter. At the top of Danniella's wish list was a car of her own. She had made the mistake of lending her previous car to Tyler and he had wrecked it. Without a car, Danniella was reliant on friends and Tyler's family to get her around, get her to work, and look after Cora. If she had a reliable car, Cora could spend the night more often. A car was the key to Danniella's freedom.

On June 17, less than two weeks after the birth of her son and just a week after she returned to work, Danniella wrote in her journal in her typical artistic style. The writing was fancy and the page was illustrated with tattoo-style pictures. She had the money for a car and was taking steps to secure the one she wanted. The entire page of her journal was filled with her dreams and goals for what came next.

Four of her goals were directly related to Cora: Get Cora's bedroom completely together; take Cora to school every day; make sure Cora is attending a sport or dance; Cora sleeping over eighty per cent of the time. Next to those goals, she had drawn a picture of a vintage-style sun and moon combined to make a female face.

Three of the goals were about getting her finances under control by paying down her bank overdraft and credit card. The other goals were personal and motivational: start school; be more positive

At the top of the page she wrote: "We need to see what the world could be, not what it is."

A CAR OF HER OWN

On Monday, July 16, 2018, Danniella was a busy lady. She had saved up enough money to finally make a down payment on a car and had some cash reserves in case of an emergency. She had found a car that was in her price range and just right for her. It was a 2014 Chevrolet Cruze, metallic dark blue that from certain angles looked almost purple.

Pearl Motors was a "buy here, pay here" dealership, which meant it specialized in older used cars with high mileage for clients with a bad credit history, providing onsite financing to purchase their vehicles. Buy here, pay here dealers often provide finance options for people who are unable to get credit elsewhere, and their loans have higher than market interest rates. The loan comes directly from the dealer and often they will stipulate repayments have to be made in person, in cash.

As Danniella was a high-risk customer, she had to make sure she had all the correct checks and paperwork in place before Pearl Motors would let her drive away.

The car was worth around $10,000 and Danniella was required to make a down payment of $1,500. She could use cash for the down payment but had to make the insurance payment via a bank transfer. Unfortunately, Danniella's bank account was overdrawn, and she would not have had enough money for both the deposit and the insurance if she were to pay back the full amount owed on her overdrawn account. She decided to deposit cash into Julie's account, from which the insurance would be paid. Then Danniella would pay the down payment on the car itself with the cash she had saved up. She requested to be allowed to pay $1,000 now, and the remaining $500 at the end of the month, then monthly repayments after that. Pearl Motors agreed to this, but as well as the usual paperwork, she needed a number of other documents, including a letter of recommendation from her landlord stating she was reliable with her rent.

Danniella had worked everything out carefully. She had a cash emergency fund, but she didn't want to touch that unless it was absolutely necessary. She planned to work double shifts to get the $500 to pay by the end of the month, but if she didn't get there, she could dip into the emergency fund. Nothing was going to stop her getting and keeping this car.

With her major goal within her reach, Danniella went back and forth all day getting everything Pearl Motors asked of her. Julie had loaned Danniella her car to do all the running around to get everything lined up so that the next day she could simply go to the yard and drive away in her very own vehicle.

When she finally got everything sorted and was approved for finance to purchase the car, she returned to

Julie's house, exhausted, in the early afternoon. It was just six weeks since she had given birth and she was still in pain. She lay down on the couch and took her painkillers, knowing she didn't have to move if she didn't want to as she was staying at Julie's that night. Julie was home alone. Her husband Patrick, son TJ and little Cora were visiting Patrick's sister in Selma, about a three-hour drive north. They had been there almost a week and were due back to Mobile in three days.

Julie and Danniella spoke of their plans for the next couple of days. The next day, Tuesday, Julie would drive Danniella to the bank and then to Pearl Motors to pick up her car. Danniella said that once she had the car, she would go shopping for some school supplies for Cora. She wanted to surprise Cora with a tie-dyed rucksack the little girl had admired. After that, Danniella planned to meet up with some friends and go out for a celebratory drink. Danniella would come back to Julie's on Thursday, when Cora and the rest of the family were due back, to surprise Cora with the rucksack and stay overnight, snuggled up with her daughter. This conversation took place while Danniella was lying on the couch, from which she barely moved once she had taken her pain relievers. She apologized to Julie for being so tired, saying: "This medicine just makes me really sleepy."

On the morning of Tuesday, July 17, 2018, Danniella rose early. All the paperwork she had needed the day before was in a large envelope that she shoved into the satchel-type handbag she always carried. It was the kind of bag that she had to dig around in for ten minutes to find anything, but everything she needed fitted in.

Julie drove Danniella to the bank, where Danniella

deposited cash into Julie's account so she could purchase the insurance for her new vehicle. Danniella was excited and busy for much of the morning, on her phone organizing everything, making sure nothing would stop her from getting her car that day. Julie smiled to see her daughter-in-law so giddy with excitement and she fervently hoped nothing would go wrong.

Julie dropped Danniella off at Pearl Motors a little after 11 a.m. Although everything should have gone smoothly, thanks to all of Danniella's organizing the previous day, Julie decided to wait out the front as Danniella signed the paperwork and got the keys just in case there was a last-minute glitch.

She needn't have worried. Ten minutes later, Danniella was finally sitting in her much-wanted car, getting the rundown of the features of the Chevy Cruze. These included a GPS that would be attached to the car, tracking all of Danniella's movements until Danniella had paid it off. The GPS plugged into a port under the steering column and pinged the car's location every four minutes. If it became disconnected, the company would receive an alert and would go in search of the car. The GPS was designed to make repossession of the car easier if a buyer failed to make their repayments. Part of the paperwork Danniella had to sign was an acknowledgment that the GPS was there, and an undertaking that she would not attempt to remove it.

Julie watched as Danniella left the car yard at 11:35 a.m., a time later confirmed by the Chevy's GPS report. She waved her daughter-in-law off and went to work.

A CELEBRATION

The rest of Danniella's day has been pieced together by the GPS data, numerous text and Facebook messages sent and received by Danniella, and eyewitness reports, as well as timestamps of phone calls and texts sent and received by friends and acquaintances that day and evening.

From the car yard, Danniella drove to her home at 701 South Apartments on University Boulevard. This journey took 24 minutes and she arrived there at 11:59am.

701 South consists of small green weatherboard apartments, ranging from studios to two bedrooms, in a complex with an onsite manager. It is in the quiet Jackson Heights neighborhood, which is considered "car dependent." There is little in walking distance, but there are supermarkets, a couple of nice gyms, restaurants, Walmart, and Home Depot all within a couple of miles. Danniella had needed to walk, catch a cab, or rely on friends to get anywhere since her last car was written off.

Now, finally, she had the freedom to come and go on a whim.

701 South is one of those places where the glossy brochures, photographs, and descriptions are far better than the reality. It is the sort of place that advertises wi-fi and a coffee bar, which could more accurately be described as a router and coffee pot in the leasing office. It could be difficult to find anyone willing to carry out maintenance when things went wrong. However, it was pet friendly, which meant Danniella could have her cat, Toulouse, and it had been freshly renovated with features such as granite countertops, black and stainless-steel kitchen appliances, hardwood flooring, and refinished cabinetry. The complex had a pool, gym, and laundry room, and was conveniently located a short walk to Medal of Honor Park, a favorite destination for playdates with Cora.

Danniella was the only person on the lease, but Tyler had his own key and the landlord was aware that he lived there when he wasn't in prison. He was in prison now, as he had given himself up after being in the hospital for the birth of Danniella's baby boy, and he wasn't due to be released for some time. It's not clear whether he would, as usual, come back to that apartment, as Danniella's journal entry suggested she was preparing her second bedroom to be Cora's room.

Danniella hadn't been going out lately, but she was determined to celebrate her new purchase that night. Being a Tuesday, she wasn't likely to find anyone who worked nine to five that would be keen for a night out drinking, but most of her friends worked in hospitality, so they might be more likely to be up for a few drinks. Also, the 89th Major League Baseball All-Star Game was on that night and would be being televised live from Washington DC Nationals Park on Fox Sports. Mobile was a baseball-mad city, having produced more baseball Hall of Famers than any other city in the US, outside of New York and Chicago. That made it more likely there would be people out and about.

Danniella remained at home for a little over five hours and in the afternoon started making plans for the evening. Just before 4:20 p.m., she texted her friend and co-worker, Hannah, to ask if she was at work, as Danniella was thinking of heading over to the mall to "get Cora's school stuff." The tie-dyed rucksack Cora wanted could be found at Target, which was in the same mall as PF Chang's.

Hannah responded: "I work at 5."

A few minutes later, Danniella sent a Facebook message to Randy Capps, who she used to work with at Hurricane's. As his bar was in the same area as her errands, she thought she might swing by for a drink to catch up. It had been a while since they had seen each other, and they weren't close enough for Danniella to have his latest number in her phone. Randy responded that he was indeed working that night, but he now worked at Heroes Bar and Grill, where she would be welcome. "Come see me," he messaged.

Danniella responded: "But I don't like going to a place I've never been before. Hurricanes is just along the way of whatever responsible things I have to get done so I can stop by and drink mid bill paying."

Randy: "Lol I hear ya. Well I'm here, not like you don't know anyone," indicating that even though Heroes was not a familiar bar to Danniella, she would at least know one person and would not be drinking alone.

At 5:20 p.m., Danniella left the house to go to the mall to look for the rucksack for Cora, and perhaps to drop in on Hannah at PF Chang's. She was casually dressed, wearing a dark shirt with the logo of the Mellow Mushroom pizza chain on the pocket. She had thrown on black leggings and black high-top Converse sneakers and tied a light-colored shirt around her waist. Her ever-changing hair was currently dark brown with red tips around the fringes, and she wore it up in a ponytail. She finished off the outfit with a pink baseball cap that had a cartoon donut sewn on the front, the type favored by Homer Simpson.

The journey should have taken no more than about ten minutes, but the GPS readout suggests that she stopped at a small strip mall on University Drive, perhaps to grab something to eat or drink at Smoothie King or pick up something from the Dollar Store or drop in to Kaoz tattoo parlor. She pulled into the carpark at The Shoppes at Bel Air at 5:50 p.m., thirty minutes after leaving home. Despite its grandiose name, the mall was just a typical large shopping center with the usual mix of department stores, specialty shops, and cafes and restaurants

PF Chang's sat on the outside of the mall, just to the right of the main entrance, with a large statue of a horse guarding its doorway. It is not clear if Danniella went into her workplace to check whether Hannah was there, but she did bump into another co-worker. The two had a brief exchange and Danniella told her how relieved she was to finally have a car. She said she couldn't stop to chat, because she was on her mission for a book bag for Cora for school.

Danniella must have gotten over her hesitation about going to an unfamiliar place, because after she left the mall, she made the eighteen-minute journey to Heroes Sports Bar and Grill where her former colleague Randy was on duty behind the bar. Perhaps she had been unable to find anyone else at the last minute on a Tuesday evening to go out for celebratory drinks.

At thirty-five, Randy was ten years older than Danniella. He had a checkered past, with arrests on felony charges, including a prison stretch for drugs and possession of stolen property. He had most recently been picked up on a DUI and drug possession charges just a few months earlier. Despite the age difference, the two must have hit it off enough that Danniella was keen to catch up.

She arrived a little after 6:30 p.m. and settled at the bar where she could chat to Randy between serving drinks. Heroes was a large, soulless sports bar, with little character in the decor, but plenty of televisions showing various sporting events. There wasn't much to attract Danniella other than the company of her friend.

They chatted about a local news story that was going semi-viral that day about a former employee of a local restaurant who had made a complaint that she had been fired after being sexually harassed by a customer. Julie had messaged Danniella about it earlier and speculated that the manager who had fired the server was someone she and Danniella had both had trouble with in the past. Randy knew the man as well and agreed that the Facebook post doing the rounds was definitely referencing Danniella's old boss.

Before long, two other people entered the bar and sat nearby. They were friends of Randy's—Denson White was in his early forties, and Mallory Miller-Kenworthy was in her mid-thirties. Denson, Mallory, and Randy all played in the same softball team. There was supposed to be a game that night, but it had been called off because of the rain. Mallory and Denson decide to go to Heroes for a drink and watch the All-Stars game, which was due to start at 7 p.m. local time. When they arrived, Randy greeted them and suggested they might like to join Danniella and keep her company. Denson, Mallory, and Danniella sat together, watching the game, and chatting to Randy while he worked behind the bar.

Danniella knew Mallory slightly. They had met in passing from time to time and had friends in the same circles. However, this was the first time that Danniella had met Denson. The three found they had something in common. Both Denson and Mallory had newborn children. Naturally, with Danniella having recently given birth too, the conversation turned to babies. Like Danniella, it was Mallory's first night out since the birth of her child six weeks earlier. When the softball game was canceled, she was determined to make the most of it.

Denson had just returned from one of his many work trips away. He had a job at Mobile Ports, a busy dock that saw 1,200 containers going in and out of the facility on an average day. Denson was a dealmaker whose work at the ports saw him receiving many honors for the city of Mobile for the business he brought to the town. His work meant he had to travel a lot and that day he still had his rental car when he arrived at Heroes.

Danniella reportedly ducked out several times, probably to have a smoke of either cigarettes or weed. She sent Julie a message at 7:14 p.m., responding to the gossip Julie had messaged about earlier: "Wow, that's so interesting cause I know its not being dramatic because I know him and that is so obvious it's him. Even Randy a bartender from downtown saw that post and he was like yeah that's 100% him."

One minute later, at 7:15 p.m., she messaged Hannah, saying: "I didn't see your car there" in reference to their earlier text conversation when Danniella told her she was heading to the mall. Hannah responded that she was, indeed, working that evening at PF Chang's.

At 7:36 p.m., Danniella messaged Hannah again, saying: "I'm drinking happily at a sports bar," to which Hannah replied at 8:09 p.m.: "Hell yes taking advantage of the freedom."

Danniella, Mallory and Denson continued to hang together and chat to Randy. At some point during the evening, the three made plans to move on to the Dublin Irish Pub and Eatery, just a little way down the road, when the game was finished. It was a fairly new bar, having opened two months earlier in a building that had previously been the much-loved Picklefish pizza and pasta joint. Dublins was a warm cozy pub with an Irish theme, live music, and a lot more atmosphere than Heroes.

They agreed to meet Randy at a third bar, Ollie's Mediterranean Grill, later that night, when Randy got off work. Ollie's was another former workplace of Danniella's and close enough to her apartment for her to walk home. Randy said he would text them to let them know when he was leaving, which he estimated would be around 11 p.m.

At 8:25 p.m. Danniella texted Hannah: "Ok I'm going to drive now but should I, I dont know." Randy would later state that Danniella had a few drinks while she was at his bar, but he didn't believe she was drunk. He claimed he would never have allowed her to drive if he thought she was over the limit, which in Alabama is 0.08 for most drivers. However, it would appear that Danniella thought she must have been touch and go. It's possible that she may have taken a couple of her painkillers, which should never be mixed with alcohol. In any event, she must have felt somewhat affected if she was questioning if she should drive.

Denson and Danniella must have hit it off. At 8:57 p.m. they became Facebook friends and Denson sent Danniella a Facebook invite to a party that was to be held at his house on August 4.

CCTV footage showed Danniella hugging Randy goodbye at 9:12 p.m. as she, Denson and Mallory left Heroes. As soon as Danniella was outside, she sent two Facebook messages to Randy. In the first, timestamped 9:12 p.m., she wrote: "You can always hang out, just let me know." A moment later, she wrote: "Ouch you saw it and didn't have response."

Randy replied to neither message.

At 9:16 p.m. Danniella attempted to call Hannah, but Hannah was working and didn't answer. She received notification of a missed call, but no message.

Later, Hannah would say she received a Snapchat video message from Danniella at 9.46 p.m. Danniella was sitting in the driver's seat of a car alone. The clip went for a few seconds and was nothing unusual or out of the ordinary enough for Hannah to remember what Danniella said, although she did think she may have been a little intoxicated. As is the case with Snapchat messages, it only played once and then self-destructed. People often use Snapchat instead of other messaging systems when they do not want records kept of their communications. Hannah said she tried to call Danniella soon after receiving the Snapchat but got no answer.

According to GPS records, Danniella's car left the Heroes parking lot at 10.05 p.m., nearly an hour after she walked out of the bar. The drive to Dublins was only half a mile, and Danniella's car arrived there at 10.08 p.m.

Denson, Mallory and Danniella continued their drinking at the Irish bar, which was popular with the college crowd. Dublins had cheap drink specials, a small stage with cheesy Irish decorations for the live music and karaoke, and a cozy outdoor area with gas heaters during winter and plenty of seating for smokers, a pool table and dart boards.

At some point, Mallory told the others that she would go to Runway Billiards, a pool hall, to meet friends before catching up with them later at Ollie's, where they had agreed to meet Randy. However, Denson told Mallory he had decided not to go to Ollie's but would rather simply head home. According to Mallory, all three of them, including Danniella, were involved in this conversation, so Danniella was aware of the change of plans.

At 10.44 pm, Randy finished work at Heroes and sent a Facebook message to Danniella that said: "I'm just getting off. About to head that way."

One minute later, at 10:45 p.m., Danniella's car left Dublins and at the same time, half a mile away, Randy left Heroes, heading toward Ollie's to meet the group as arranged earlier. Denson and Mallory each left Dublins in separate cars at the same time as Danniella.

Randy arrived at Ollie's at 10:48 p.m., three minutes later, looked around for his friends, and then at 10:50 p.m. he called Mallory. At 10:57 p.m. Randy called Denson, who didn't answer. Randy settled in to wait for the others to arrive.

When leaving Dublins, anyone who was going to Runway, as Mallory was, or to Ollie's, as the plan originally was, would turn left after leaving the parking lot. The route to Ollie's takes you back past Heroes and then it is just another three- or four-minute drive in a straight line to get to Runway.

If Denson was heading home, he would have turned right and kept going—in the opposite direction of both Ollie's and Runway.

The GPS data shows Danniella's car going right when she left Dublins. This was confirmed by Mallory, who stated that she turned left, toward Runway, and saw both Denson and Danniella head in the opposite direction. Mallory was aware Denson was going home, so his turn made sense, but Mallory had no idea why Danniella did so. Still, she wasn't a close friend, so she didn't think much of it.

Danniella knew the area and the venues very well. Regardless of whether she was going to Ollie's to meet Randy, or following Mallory to Runway, she would have turned left when she left the parking lot. Even if Danniella was tipsy, her familiarity with the area meant there was no chance of confusion. Instead, she turned right, following Denson's car.

Denson would later reportedly say that he did not know that Danniella was following him. However, after around fifteen minutes, when the cars were passing through a quiet non-residential industrial area, Danniella flashed her lights at Denson, indicating he should pull over. Although there were open gas stations nearby, as well as a well-lit Waffle House, the two cars pulled into a dark, closed Shell gas station on Government Drive at 11:05 p.m. Once they stopped, Danniella told Denson that she had lost her phone.

At 11:07 p.m., the GPS in Danniella's car made its final location call.

The type of GPS installed by Pearl Motors was one that plugged into an outlet underneath the steering wheel. The location is slightly different in each model of car, although a quick Google search will tell you where it is for a specific model. By law, Pearl Motors had to inform Danniella that it was there. It is a simple matter to unplug the GPS if you know where it is, but it is not something that will come out accidentally. Once the GPS is out, it stops sending locations back to the base. Pearl Motors would be quickly advised that it had stopped pinging.

It appeared that Danniella tried searching her car for her phone and that Denson rang the phone via Facebook Messenger, presumably to try and locate it. Why he called via Facebook rather than using her telephone number isn't clear, but friends later speculated that she had not memorized her own phone number as she had a habit of losing or otherwise changing phones. Also, as she was a bit tipsy after a night of drinking, the chances are she couldn't tell him the right number. When they couldn't hear a tone, Danniella assumed she must have left the phone at Dublins.

At 11:17 p.m. Denson called Randy, who was sitting at Ollie's with Mallory who had arrived five minutes earlier. The two of them were waiting for Danniella to show up as arranged. Randy was a regular at Ollie's and usually sat at the bar or on the front patio. He was outside smoking when Mallory arrived, and she had to call him to find out where he was. Denson told Randy that he was going back to Dublins to find Danniella's phone.

At 11:24 p.m. the two cars left the gas station and turned left toward the interstate. Denson returned to Dublins as planned, and Danniella followed for a bit before the two cars went separate ways. Danniella's car headed to a more populated part of town.

At 11:37 p.m. Denson sent Mallory a photo message with a selfie of himself sitting at the bar at Dublins. In the picture, Denson is holding his hand up with his thumb to his ear and pinky finger pointing at his mouth, in the universal symbol to indicate telephone use. Underneath the picture he wrote: "Getting phone."

In a second message straight below that, he wrote: "Just got back here. But somehow lost Danniella."

A server at Dublins had found the phone on the trunk of a car when she was leaving work and brought it in to put it behind the bar. Denson was able to retrieve Danniella's phone from the bartender and at 11:52 p.m. he called her via Facebook Messenger again. It is not clear why Denson tried to contact Danniella in this way, when he had her phone and she presumably had no way of getting the call. When there was no answer, he wrote a

Facebook message that said: "Call me!! Dublin had your phone."

At approximately midnight, Denson arrived at Ollie's, apparently having decided not to head straight home after all. When Randy and Mallory told him Danniella had not shown up, he tried calling her via Facebook video a couple more times, at 12:04 a.m. and 12:33 a.m. After getting no response, he asked the only person who was friends with Danniella, Randy, what he should do with her phone. Randy suggested he take it to PF Chang's the next day, so Danniella could be reunited with it on her next shift.

Denson left Ollie's and then, somewhat curiously, decided to return his rental car to the rental agency at around 1 a.m. We can speculate that the car hire place he used was the one on Airport Boulevarde, nearby Ollie's, which had a facility to drop keys into a drop box and return the hire car at any time of day or night. Denson may have left his own car there and taken the opportunity to swap back to it. From there, Denson went home to his wife and children, still holding on to Danniella's phone.

MISSING PERSON

At approximately 7:30 a.m. on the morning of Wednesday, July 18, Hannah realized she hadn't heard from Danniella since the message she had received saying she wasn't sure she was all right to drive. Hannah shot off a text message, saying: "You good?" She didn't expect a response right away after Danniella's big night out and went about her day.

At exactly the same time, Julie Thomas received a call from a man who introduced himself as Denson White and said he had found Danniella's phone. Julie thought the man had merely found a phone of someone he didn't know, not that he was a friend of Danniella's. Julie didn't think much of it. Danniella was always losing her phone. Julie told Denson the same thing Randy had: he should drop the phone off at Danniella's work, PF Chang's. Meanwhile, Julie arranged for the building supervisor to put a note on Danniella's front door saying she knew where her phone was.

Denson did not take the phone to PF Chang's as

suggested by both Randy and Julie. Instead, he called Julie a few more times over the next couple of days, expressing concern about Danniella. Julie had no idea who Denson was, but she assured him that everything was going to be all right. Eventually she told him: "You just hang onto it, and when Danniella gets in touch I'll let you know and we can figure it out from there. We'll see what Danniella wants to do."

By Thursday evening, when Danniella did not show up to see her daughter, Julie became worried. She contacted her daughter-in-law's friend Hannah through Facebook and asked her if she had heard anything.

Hearing from Julie triggered an alarm in Hannah. She realized she had never received a response to the last text message she had sent Danniella. Hannah tried to text her again and got no response. She tried messaging her on Facebook Messenger but got no response there either.

Feeling something was very wrong, Hannah started messaging mutual friends and received a response from one that Danniella had said she was going to Heroes on the Tuesday night. Hannah recalled that Danniella mentioned she had been at a sports bar, and Heroes fit the bill.

Hannah called Heroes and asked the manager to check the parking lot for a blue Chevy Cruze. Hannah was able to describe the car clearly because she had taken it for a test drive a few days earlier, as she was a more confident driver than Danniella. The manager reported that no car matching that description was in the parking lot and offered to check who had been working that night. The manager called Hannah back to advise her that the barman on duty, Randy Capps, confirmed that Danniella had been there that night, hanging out with Denson and Mallory.

With such a unique name, Hannah was soon able to track Denson down through Facebook as a new friend of Danniella's. She sent him a Facebook message at 9:17 p.m. on Thursday, July 19 that said: "Hey I'm Danniella's friend, we haven't heard from her since Tuesday night and we are all very concerned, if you know where she could be at, or have any information please message me back."

Denson called Hannah that night. He told her that he had Danniella's phone and had been trying to return it to her. He said he had not seen her since Tuesday night.

Hannah told Denson she was going to drive by Danniella's apartment that night and he asked Hannah to let him know if she was there. She went to the apartment and found no sign of Danniella. Hannah sent more messages to Danniella on Facebook saying, "Hey what's up, everybody's worried."

Driving by Danniella's apartment the next morning on her way to cosmetology school, it was clear Danniella had not been home. Hannah decided to drop into PF Chang's to see if Danniella had reported to her 10 a.m. shift. She hadn't. Hannah called Julie and messaged Denson to let them know that there was still no sign of Danniella.

There was a flurry of telephone calls and messages between Julie, Hannah, and Denson that Friday morning as they decided it was definitely time to go to the police station and report Danniella missing. The last anyone had heard from her was Tuesday, and although it was not unusual for a fun-loving 25-year-old to be out of contact for a day or two, missing work and not showing up to greet her daughter were both major red flags when it came to Danniella.

Julie and Denson made plans to meet at the police station, where Julie could file a missing person's report and Denson could hand over the phone and make a statement. Along with Julie's husband, Patrick, they met up at the police headquarters on the corner of Airport Boulevard and Dawes. Denson handed over Danniella's phone and gave Julie a quick rundown of what had transpired the previous Tuesday night.

They soon discovered they were at the wrong police station and were instructed to go to the office on Government Street where the missing persons liaison unit was located. On the way, Julie called Hannah to ask if she knew the six-digit number to unlock Daniella's phone. Hannah said it was Danniella's employee number. Julie dropped into PF Chang's before going to the second police station to get her daughter-in-law's employee number, and she and Patrick read through the text messages Danniella had sent and received during the past week, as well as listening to her voicemail.

Because of Julie and Patrick's detour, Denson arrived at the second police station before them. By the time Julie arrived, Denson was just finishing giving his statement to the police. Hannah also came down to make a statement about how unlike Danniella it was to be out of contact for so long, and especially not to show for her shift at a time when she needed the money most.

Julie provided as much information as she could and surrendered the phone to the police. A police officer later accompanied her to Danniella's apartment, where a crime scene officer met them. Nothing seemed out of the ordinary, missing or out of place.

Back at home, Julie logged on to her computer, where Danniella had saved her own login details to various social media, including Facebook. Concern for Danniella's wellbeing overcame her reluctance to violate her privacy. With TJ's help, Julie logged into Danniella's Facebook account so they could read through her messages and search for clues. Using her Facebook Messenger and what they had noted down from her phone records before handing Danniella's cell phone to police, they pieced together as best they could what happened on the Tuesday night she went missing.

Among the Facebook messages were several missed calls from Denson White's account. A voicemail message had been left at 11:11 p.m. on the night Danniella was last seen. It was clear that the message was left accidentally, as two voices were muttering in the background. One was Danniella, sounding like she was slurring her words, and the other was presumably Denson. A minute later, the same thing happened. It was a Facebook message at 11:12 p.m. from Denson's account, that he apparently was unaware he was leaving. The male voice cried out, "Woah careful … Don't touch that," or something similar. There was a hint of a muffled female voice in the background. A few minutes earlier, Danniella's GPS pinged for the last time.

Julie called the police to tell them what they had found in Danniella's Facebook. The police advised her not to log back into her account again, as doing so might taint the evidence.

Julie checked back with the police often. She

wondered about CCTV footage from the various places that they knew Danniella had been that night, but the police advised her that no CCTV footage had been found, including from the Shell where the last confirmed sighting had been. Julie was shocked when a news outlet reporting on Danniella's disappearance featured CCTV footage from the Shell gas station. It showed a car, presumed to be Danniella's, pull in, and another car pull in beside it a few seconds later. As the service station was closed, the cameras were activated by motion sensors. The surveillance was activated at 11:05 p.m., the same time that Daniella's GPS recorded her car arriving there. A couple of minutes later, the second car left and then immediately after, either a third car pulled in or the second car returned.

The footage was grainy and appeared to be nearly useless. No people could be made out in it. It was impossible to tell if the second car had left and returned, or if a different car came after the second car left. Julie called the police and demanded to know why the footage was on TV when they had told her none existed. Rather than responding, law enforcement officials contacted the news station demanding the footage be removed, citing that it put Danniella in "danger." The news outlet complied, but no further reasons for the police action were given.

CUSTODY

Less than a week after Danniella was last seen, Julie and Patrick Thomas attended court to finalize custody arrangements for Cora. Cora had been living with her grandparents for some time, and Danniella had previously agreed that the custody arrangements should be formalized, giving the little girl much-needed stability.

Julie claimed that Danniella was worried that somebody would decide that, because of Tyler's circumstances and their living arrangement, Danniella should not have custody of Cora. She said Danniella was happy to sign over full-time custody of Cora to them until she could stabilize herself and get her life into order. It was clear from Danniella's journal that she hoped to regain custody sooner rather than later, with the entries about getting Cora's bedroom ready for her and having Cora sleep over most nights.

The custody process had been going on for some months and was all but completed. The paperwork was signed and filed, and all the meetings had been attended. The court date that was the final step in formalizing Cora's custody arrangements was set for Tuesday, July 24. Danniella didn't show up and Julie and Patrick were awarded custody in absentia.

The next day, eight days after Danniella's disappearance, Tyler got out of prison and returned to the apartment he shared with Danniella. He immediately took the few things of value, including the gaming system and television, and pawned them. Upon discovering this, Julie bought back the items that had belonged to Danniella.

That day, the Mobile police also confirmed that the case had been handed over to homicide. This was a hugely unusual thing to do barely a week after a missing persons report had been filed, but they made a statement that although homicide detectives had taken over the case, there was no evidence that a homicide had occurred. As far as anyone knew, there had been no new evidence that suggested Danniella had been murdered.

Police who were monitoring Danniella's bank account activity were alerted when they received notification that her Visa debit card had been used at a gas station. PF Chang's paid her with Visa debit cards so that her money didn't go into her bank account, which was overdrawn. However, this information just led back to Tyler, who had found the debit card with just a few dollars on it when he had gone through the apartment.

Hannah also went through Danniella's apartment on Friday, July 27—the same day that a vigil was held for Danniella. The police had already been through, and Tyler gave her the key, asking her if she could spot anything unusual or out of place, as she had been a frequent recent visitor to the apartment. All Danniella's stuff was still there, including make-up, around $60 in cash, clothes and her phone charger. It was not the scene of someone who had run away.

According to the whiteboard on which Danniella kept track of her goals and the amount of money she had saved, there should have been around $1200 she had put aside. If that money was in the apartment, no official record of it being found exists.

There was no chance Tyler would be able to maintain payments on the apartment alone. With Danniella the only person on the lease, the rent was soon in arrears and she was officially evicted from the apartment. The complex management would not allow Julie into the apartment to collect Danniella's possessions, but dumped them unceremoniously on the pavement, letting Julie know she could come and collect them if she wanted. Julie went straight over to pick up everything Danniella owned.

Julie and Tyler went through all Danniella's belongings. There were no clues among them at all. Pearl Motors had not been able to track the location of the car, and no vehicle matching its description had been reported as abandoned. Danniella Vian and her new Chevy Cruze had apparently vanished into thin air.

LEADS AND QUESTIONS

On Friday, September 14, Mobile Police responded to a complaint at a home about 15 miles southwest of Mobile in Wigfield Road in Theodore, Alabama. Due to reports of violence and potentially armed suspects, police swooped on the house in a raid that included a helicopter, an armored vehicle and ground controls.

After a dramatic and noisy entry by armed police, three people were detained. Later, one of them, thirty-six-year-old Jason Corey Dykes, was arrested on charges of domestic violence, strangulation, assault, and unlawful imprisonment. He had been accused of locking a former girlfriend in a room, beating, and raping her.

Jason Dykes was the nephew of Julie and cousin of Tyler. According to multiple sources, the alleged victim claimed that Jason had said something threatening enough about Danniella Vian that it "raised red flags" for law enforcement. Police sent in the K9 squad and a large contingent of new recruits to search the surrounding area to determine whether there was any sign of Danniella on the property. However, the raid came up with nothing and police determined that Jason Dykes' crimes had no relation to Danniella's disappearance.

JULIE THOMAS RAN A GOFUNDME CAMPAIGN, and used the money raised for flyers that she handed out around town and put into letterboxes in the area, as well as billboards featuring Danniella's photo and details about her disappearance.

Just before Christmas, a frustrated Hannah Jakoboski left a one-star review on the Mobile Police Department's Facebook page. "Danniella Vian has been missing for 5 months," she wrote. "5 months her baby girl hasn't seen her mom. 5 months Danniella hasn't gotten to hold her daughter. 5 months her family has had to sit around and wonder when will we all get answers. Danniella Vian went missing July 17 2018. The mobile police department know who she was with last, seen on video surveillance but they say they have ran out of leads?

"It's crazy that MPD will post about robberies, stolen property and post surveillance videos asking for help but not for Danniella. They post about awards police officers are receiving but can't post one missing picture of Danniella. They should hand out awarded to police officers that find missing people not stolen property.

"Danniella was stolen. A person was stolen not some groceries, a person. I have lost all faith in the mobile police department. I have hope that some way or another Danniella and all the missing girls from mobile will be found but it won't be from the help of the mobile police department. They sweep the missing under the rug."

NOWHERE TO BE FOUND

As the months churned on, Julie never lost hope of finding Danniella, maintaining a presence on forums that were dedicated to finding the missing mother, even when the comments were cruel or unnecessary.

There were many theories put forward by those close to Danniella, as well as internet sleuths who became obsessed with the details of the disappearance. These ranged from Danniella running away to start a new life, to accidentally running her car into a body of water, to committing suicide. The more sinister theories were that she was the victim of a carjacking gone wrong, that she went to buy drugs and was attacked, and that she was deliberately targeted to settle a drug debt. On the extreme end, some people even speculated that she was a victim of Alabama's sex trafficking trade. However, no evidence emerged to definitively support any of the many theories.

The three people who were the last known to see Danniella—Denson White, Mallory Miller-Kenworthy and Randy Capps—elected not to provide any statements to media, although all three were cooperative with police. Everyone close to Danniella, including Julie, Tyler, and Hannah, as well as the three who were with her that night, agreed to take polygraph tests. The outcome of those tests is unknown.

If the information passed on by Danniella to Julie about her right to reverse her decision to adopt out her baby boy for up to six months was correct, then the adoption presumably became permanent on December 6, 2018.

Several vigils were held for Danniella. Her friends and family were determined she would not be forgotten and kept pressure on police to not stop the search. On March 8, 2019, when Danniella should have turned twenty-six, another vigil was held by the playgrounds at Medal of Honor Park. Attendance was low compared to previous vigils, with only one member of the media in attendance.

It was the first vigil that Hannah didn't come to. Tyler and Randy both attended, but Julie kept Cora away as she didn't want the little girl associating birthdays with sadness. Around twenty family and friends held cupcakes, a prayer was said and then the vigil candles were used to light the candles on the cupcakes as family and friends sang: "Happy Birthday Danniella. Happy Birthday to you."

FOUND

On May 2, 2019, a law enforcement dive team was on a training mission in Bayou Sara in Saraland when they came across a submerged car. Upon closer inspection, divers noted what appeared to be a body in the front seat of the car. They called in the details. The make and model matched the car belonging to Danniella Vian.

The next day, a crew pulled the car out of the water and the body was determined to be that of an adult female. A few weeks later, forensic testing confirmed the woman was Danniella Vian.

The Mobile Police Department drained the car completely looking for further evidence, but eventually ruled the cause of death "undetermined." They stated that how the car was found was "consistent with that of an accident." The spot where Danniella's car had gone into the water was a gentle slope that continued on from the road and could have been easily missed in the dark by someone who was not familiar with the area.

Those closest to Danniella were not convinced that Danniella's death was an accident and they tried to keep the investigation open. They pointed out that Danniella had no reason to be in the area where she was found. There were still unanswered questions about her GPS being disabled. However, although the case was not officially closed, the Mobile Police Department no longer treated it as an active investigation.

On June 30, 2020, Danniella's car was posted for sale on the internet. It was sold to a Ukrainian bidder for $25, with no mention of the body that had been removed from it. Julie took to Facebook with her frustration, posting: "We're under the impression that the investigation is still open n active n then find this!! Is this not evidence? Or a potential crime scene? This makes no sense..especially when her family..her daughter hasn't been given any kind of update!!"

On March 10, 2021, Julie posted on the Alabama Crime Watch Network: "I'm reaching out … I want to talk to Denson White. I want to hear Your side of what happened that night with Danniella Vian. What you've told me when we filed her report doesn't add up. You gave your statement to the police and then just disappeared. You have the answers that will help us find out what happened to her. If anyone knows Denson, will you please forward this to him? Please share …"

To this day, Julie and Hannah continue to keep Danniella's memory alive, organizing vigils every year and making media appearances imploring anyone who knows more about Danniella's fateful last hours to come forward. They say they will not give up until the case is solved. They need the closure to determine whether it was mishap... or murder.

MORE BOOKS AND FREEBIES

Keep going for sneak peeks of more books and to find out how to get your FREE TRUE CRIME BOOK

A MANUAL FOR MURDER

THE TRUE STORY OF HOW A BOOK LED TO A TRIPLE HOMICIDE

When officers attend a triple homicide in a well-to-do neighborhood in Maryland, it looks like a robbery gone wrong. But why did the intruder kill a profoundly disabled boy who had no way of identifying him?

When the FBI is called in, their investigations take them from the glamorous world of Hollywood music royalty to the seediest districts of Detroit. It looks like the killer might have been too smart for them, until they find a book in a suspect's apartment, which may be the key to unraveling it all.

GET THIS EXCLUSIVE EBOOK AT EILEENORMSBY.COM

This book is not for sale and is only available to those who sign up for my newsletter. But don't worry: I won't spam you or pass your information on to anyone else. You can unsubscribe any time you like, even right after you download your free book! I don't mind, though I do hope you will stick around for updates to the cases I write about and to be first to know about any new books

PSYCHO.COM
SERIAL KILLERS ON THE INTERNET

True tales of serial killers who went viral

Serial killers have been with us for decades. The internet has put them in our pockets

The Dnepropetrovsk Maniacs: A pair of teens go on a murderous spree, filming themselves along the way. When their deadly rampage is finished, more than 20 are dead and their exploits are immortalized in the most shocking video ever to circulate the internet, "**3 Guys, 1 Hammer**"

Pedro Rodrigues Filho, aka "Killer Petey": A serial killer with over 100 kills to his name prides himself on killing only murderers, rapists and pedophiles. When he walks free, he becomes a Youtube sensation

Mark Twitchell, aka the "Dexter" Serial Killer: A psychopath lures victims through online dating to use as "research" for his twisted film project

Psycho.com is a chilling look at what happens when murderous minds meet modern technology.

"What I loved most about the book is it wasn't just about the killers and what made them tick, but also focused on the victims who deserved to be remembered just as much if not more" - reviewer

HEAD TO EILEENORMSBY.COM FOR BUYING OPTIONS

MURDER ON THE DARK WEB

TRUE STORIES FROM THE DARK SIDE OF THE INTERNET

A look into the dark side of the internet's secret underbelly

A Minnesota dog trainer is found dead of an apparent suicide after detectives find her details on a dark web murder-for-hire site. But who paid $13,000 in Bitcoin to kill this devout Christian and beloved wife and mother?

An Instagram glamour model is drugged, kidnapped and listed for sale on a dark web human trafficking site. A secret society called Black Death demands a ransom for her safe return, or else she will be sold to sadistic millionaires to use before feeding to the tigers.

The dark web is the internet's evil twin, where anything can be bought and sold. Drugs, weapons, and hackers-for-hire are available at the touch of a button.

Most who visit merely look around, happy to simply satisfy their curiosity before leaving, never to return. But some are sucked into the criminal underworld and find themselves doing things they would never have contemplated in the real world—ordering a hit on a love rival or bidding on an auction for a sex slave—like the people in this book.

These are extraordinary true tales of infidelity, betrayal and shadowy hitmen and human traffickers who may not be that they seem.

HEAD TO EILEENORMSBY.COM FOR BUYING OPTIONS

STALKERS
TRUE TALES OF DEADLY OBSESSIONS

Deluded narcissists. Obsessed fans. Sinister internet trolls. Stalkers who turned deadly

A Hollywood starlet on a smash-hit sitcom enjoys rising fame, unaware that her greatest fan is hell-bent on meeting his crush. When she films a love scene, his adoration turns into a quest to see her punished

A gameshow winner turns to writing books. When one is given a scathing review, he tracks down the reviewer with bloody results

A teenage boy enjoys online chatrooms. When he meets a sexy Secret Service operative, she convinces him he has been chosen to be a spy with a licence to kill... and his first target is his own best friend.

Men keep turning up at a newlywed's home convinced that she has placed a Craigslist ad for a rough fantasy roleplay. Things turn violent before police are able to unravel a twisted and diabolical scheme

STALKERS takes you into the twisted world of cyberstalking, catfishing, rejected suitors, jealous exes and celebrity stalkers, and the devastating impact their obsessions can have on their victims. This is a standalone book in the Dark Webs True Crime series. It is not necessary to have read the others in the series

LITTLE GIRLS LOST
TRUE TALES OF HEINOUS CRIMES

Four shocking crimes. Four lives lost. Countless lives shattered.

True stories of young lives cut brutally short that will make you want to hug your daughter and never let her go.

⚠ **Note: this is a true crime book that contains descriptions of sexual violence against children. Reader discretion is advised**

An 11-year-old girl never makes it home from a Halloween party. When the people of the tight-knit Oil City discover what was done to her, they cancel Halloween until the real monsters who roam their streets can be caught.

A 14-year-old girl is excited to attend her first evening party with local teens. What happens there is every parent's nightmare, but it is made infinitely worse when the residents of the town close ranks around the perpetrators.

A schoolgirl comes to the aid of a middle-aged woman who has lost her puppy and becomes the victim of the most hated couple in Australian history.

Police tell gang members a 16-year-old girl has agreed to testify against them, with predictable results. When they make an arrest for her murder, a Hollywood sitcom plays a surprising role in the outcome

HEAD TO EILEENORMSBY.COM FOR BUYING OPTIONS

THE DARKEST WEB

The Darkest Web

Dark...

A kingpin willing to murder to protect his dark web drug empire. A corrupt government official determined to avoid exposure. The death of a dark web drugs czar in mysterious circumstances in a Bangkok jail cell, just as the author arrives there.

Who is Variety Jones and why have darknet markets ballooned tenfold since authorities shut down the original dark web drugs bazaar, Silk Road? Who are the kingpins willing to sell poisons and weapons, identities and bank accounts, malware and life-ruining services online to anyone with a wallet full of Bitcoin?

Darker...

A death in Minnesota leads detectives into the world of dark web murder-for-hire where hundreds of thousands of dollars in Bitcoin is paid to arrange killings, beatings and rapes. Meanwhile, the owner of the most successful hitman website in history is threatening the journalists who investigate his business with a visit from his operatives - and the author is at the top of his list.

Darkest...

People with the most depraved perversions gather to share their obscene materials in an almost inaccessible corner of the dark web. A video circulates and the pursuit of the monsters responsible for 'Daisy's Destruction' lead detectives into the unimaginable horror of the world of hurtcore.

There's the world wide web - the internet we all know that connects us via news, email, forums, shopping and social media. Then there's the dark web - the parallel internet accessed by only a select few. Usually, those it connects wish to remain anonymous and for good reason.

Eileen Ormsby has spent the past five years exploring every corner of the Dark Web. She has shopped on darknet markets, contributed to forums, waited in red rooms and been threatened by hitmen on murder-for-hire sites. On occasions, her dark web activities have poured out into the real world and she has attended trials, met with criminals and the law enforcement who tracked them down, interviewed dark web identities and visited them in prison.

This book will take you into the murkiest depths of the web's dark underbelly: a place of hitmen for hire, red rooms, hurtcore sites and markets that will sell anything a person is willing to pay for - including another person. The Darkest Web.

Published by Allen & Unwin

HEAD TO EILEENORMSBY.COM FOR BUYING OPTIONS

SILK ROAD

It was the 'eBay of drugs', a billion dollar empire. Behind it was the FBI's Most Wanted Man, a mysterious crime czar dubbed 'Dread Pirate Roberts'. SILK ROAD lay at the heart of the 'Dark Web' - a parallel internet of porn, guns, assassins and drugs. Lots of drugs. With the click of a button LSD, heroin, meth, coke, any illegal drug imaginable, would wing its way by regular post from any dealer to any user in the world. How was this online drug cartel even possible? And who was the mastermind all its low roads led to? This is the incredible true story of Silk Road's rise and fall, told with unparalleled insight into the main players - including alleged founder and kingpin Dread Pirate Roberts himself - by lawyer and investigative journalist Eileen Ormsby. A stunning crime story with a truth that explodes off the page.

Published by Pan MacMillan

HEAD TO EILEENORMSBY.COM FOR BUYING OPTIONS

FROM THE AUTHOR

Thank you for giving me your valuable time to share these stories with you.

A great deal of work goes into researching these crimes and writing about them in a way that gives voice to the victims. The most important part of how well a book sells is how many positive reviews it has, so if you leave me one then you are directly helping me to continue to report on these stories for you.

Just a line or two is all it takes to make an author's day.

SEARCH FOR "MISHAP OR MURDER?" ON AMAZON OR GOODREADS TO LEAVE YOUR REVIEW

Thank you so much.

Printed in Great Britain
by Amazon